IMAGES
of Sport

CHESTER CITY
FOOTBALL CLUB

Ray Gill holds the record for most Football League appearances by a Chester player. A steady and consistent left-back, Gill played 406 League and 43 cup games between 1951 and 1962, including 112 successive League games between 1952 and 1954. He joined Chester from Manchester City in June 1951 and scored on his debut, against Wrexham, on 18 August 1951. This goal proved to be only one of three League goals he scored for Chester. Gill played his final game for the club, at the age of thirty-seven, against Carlisle United on the closing day of the 1961/62 season. After leaving Sealand Road, he played Cheshire County League football for Hyde United and Altrincham.

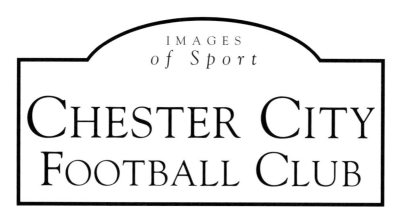

IMAGES
of Sport

CHESTER CITY
FOOTBALL CLUB

Compiled by
Chas Sumner

TEMPUS

First published 2002
Copyright © Chas Sumner, 2002

Tempus Publishing Limited
The Mill, Brimscombe Port,
Stroud, Gloucestershire, GL5 2QG

ISBN 0 7524 2420 3

Typesetting and origination by
Tempus Publishing Limited
Printed in Great Britain by
Midway Colour Print, Wiltshire

The players relax outside the Norbreck Hydro Hotel in Blackpool before the FA Cup tie against Newcastle United in January 1966. Left-half Dave Durie, who was also a Methodist Sunday School teacher in Blackpool, entertains the players on his guitar. From left to right: George Evans, Gary Talbot, Tommy Singleton, Dennis Reeves, Mike Metcalf, Fred Willder.

Contents

A packed Spion Kop for Sealand Road's largest attendance, in January 1952, against Chelsea in the FA Cup.

Acknowledgements

It would have been impossible to compile this book without the help of a large number of people and I am extremely grateful to everyone who loaned me items and gave me permission to use them in this collection.

I would particularly like to thank Nick Harrison and the staff of the *Chester Evening Leader* for allowing me access to their collection of more recent photographs, as well as Ian Bedford at the *Chester Chronicle*. Both Nick and Ian have always been extremely supportive of my requests to reproduce their photographs.

I would also like to thank Giles Park and CM Pixel8 for their photographic expertise, and Steve Mansley and Richard Prince for their suggestions and advice.

Thanks should also go to the following, who have assisted by supplying photographs or memorabilia: Pete Bishop, Karl Brownbill, Cheshire Record Office, Rob Clegg, Chris Courtenay-Williams, Alec Croft, Cumbrian Newspapers Ltd (Penrith action photograph), Steve Cunnington, Gareth M. Davies, Ken Evans, Gary Greatorex, Barrie Hipkiss, Michael and Sheelagh Horne, Jane Jago, Ray Jones, Stuart Mason, Dorothy Mercer, Mike Metcalf, Grenville Millington, Arthur Morris, Olwen Oliver, Jean Pritchard, Jacqueline Rainsforth, David Sallery (train photograph), Barry Sands, Tim Savidge, Dan Skitt, Gary Talbot, Alan Trotter, Sheila Yates. Sincere apologies to anyone I have inadvertently omitted from this list.

Finally, I would like to thank my wife Diane for once again being very patient while I spent many hours on this latest project.

Introduction

It has never been easy supporting Chester City and the last few years have tested the resolve of the most ardent City fan. For any supporter who started watching the club after the move to the Deva Stadium in 1992, it has been a particularly painful experience. In the last ten years, supporters have experienced four different owners, twelve months in administration, as well as three relegations – including the disastrous drop out of the Football League in 2000, when the club were less than half an hour from safety. In addition there have been twelve different managers, a remarkable figure when you take into consideration the fact that one of them, Kevin Ratcliffe, was in charge for almost half that time.

Many would argue that this has always been the case. After all, the club almost folded in 1897 due to financial problems and, in a remarkable parallel to the departure from Sealand Road in 1990, they were forced to leave the Old Showground in 1899 with no alternative home venue available. It certainly would be interesting to know the thoughts of fans from the Victorian era as to the club's recent problems. However, despite many years of struggle there have been numerous occasions to savour.

Compiling this book has certainly brought back memories for me, not all of them good, but every image has acted as a reminder of what it is like to be a Chester City supporter. Seeing the photographs of fans crying on the pitch after the Peterborough game in May 2000 may bring back feelings of anger at the circumstances behind relegation, but they also act as a wonderful reminder of how important this club is to so many people.

I saw my first game at Sealand Road in 1967 and my main recollection of that game is hearing the crowd chant 'Sack Hauser' as Chester lost 3-1. It took many years before I realised what an important contribution Peter Hauser made to the club's history by creating one of the most attractive sides to represent the city in 1964/65. It certainly shows how fickle fans can be and makes me regret that I was too young to see that side in action. The photographs from the mid-1960s certainly show a team that enjoyed their football and the former chairman, Reg Rowlands, must take a lot of credit for creating such a happy atmosphere. The players that I have spoken to from that era clearly held Reg in high regard and it is to his great credit that they all thought of him as 'one of the lads'. You feel that a true Blue like Reg would have been particularly distressed by the events of the last few years.

The 1970s produced some great memories, most notably an appearance in the League Cup semi-final in the 1974/75 season. I still believe that the 3-0 victory over League Champions Leeds United in the fourth round should be regarded as one of the greatest giant-killing acts of all-time. In these days of blanket television coverage, the goals would have been replayed time

The author pictured with the 1964/65 forward line that scored 116 of the team's 119 League goals. From left to right: Elfed Morris, Mike Metcalf, the author, Hugh Ryden, Gary Talbot, Jimmy Humes.

and time again, but now we only have photographs and newspaper cuttings to remind us of that great win. Seeing the picture of John 'Jesse' James scoring the first goal in that game still brings a tingle to the spine.

The 1980s saw the emergence of Stuart Rimmer and promotion, in 1985/86, under Harry McNally. In the first half of that season, Stuart was unstoppable and everything he touched turned to gold until his unfortunate injury against Orient. McNally himself is a legend at Chester and you could always rely on one of Harry's teams to forge a result when it was most needed. The photograph of Harry at Bradford City truly sums up the man in my eyes, simmering with discontent after seeing two of his players sent off in the first forty-five minutes. Many players and referees received a verbal lashing from the man, but he will always be remembered for the wonderful job he did avoiding relegation while in exile at Macclesfield.

As for the Sealand Road ground, it was a sad day when the players walked off the pitch for the last time after victory over Rotherham United in April 1990. All that is left now is a nondescript retail park, but you can't help feeling that an excellent opportunity to develop both the ground and area was wasted by everyone concerned. Looking at the photographs of the Chester ground when they entered the League in 1931, it is interesting to note that sixty years later the Sealand Road End still looked virtually the same while the Spion Kop, which was banked in the mid-1930s, remained uncovered.

I hope that these images evoke a sense of nostalgia. What of the future? Who knows what it will bring. One thing is for certain, it's about time our great club had a change in fortune – it's long overdue.

Chas Sumner,
March 2002

One
Pre-League Days
1885-1931

Chester Football Club were formed in 1885 as an amalgamation of Chester Rovers and King's School Old Boys. This 1884/85 group shows the Chester Rovers team that featured many players who went on to form the new side. From left to right, back row: J. Hack, G. James, Lythgoe, W. Thrash, J. Southworth, -?-. Front row: McMillan, A.C. Lockwood, J. Tomkinson, Banks, S. Jones. James Southworth, a conductor of the orchestra at the Royalty Theatre in Chester, went on to win an FA Cup winner's medal with Blackburn Rovers. His brother, John, also played for Chester, in their early years, as a goalkeeper but was later awarded 3 England international caps as an outfield player.

OSWESTRY *V.* CHESTER.

The football season was opened at Oswestry on Saturday, on the Cricket Ground. Victoria-road. The competing teams were Oswestry Town and Chester City. The home team kicked off soon after half-past two o'clock, and in less than five minutes J. Davies drew first blood for them. McMillan and Lockwood had several runs down their wing, but they were well checked by Powell, who played effectively throughout the game. Groves managed to elude Isaac Jones at back, and shot the ball into the home goal, but Davies was on the alert, and threw the ball out. Joseph Davies scored the second goal for the home team from a well-directed shot. One of the home forwards handled the ball, and from the kick it was put in the Oswestry goal, but Davies relieved his citadel. Bryan and Roach dribbled nicely down their wing, and the former took a shot at the visitors' goal, the ball striking the cross-bar, and after rebounding into play Pierce managed to elude the goalkeeper, and scored the third goal for his side Bryan became dangerous and just missed a goal. A Cestrian handled the leather, and Powell was entrusted with the kick. He placed the ball well in the mouth of the visitors' goal, but it was kicked behind. J E. Davies afterwards sent the ball over the bar. Davies. the home goalkeeper, was again called upon, the ball having been sent into his hands. Before he could get rid of it three or four of the Cestrians bore upon him, and a goal seemed inevitable. Davies fell, and in the scuffle managed to throw out the leather, and thus relieved his citadel. J. E. Davies made some good attempts at scoring, after which half-time was called. On the resumption of hostilities, the Cestrians seemed to be defeated on every point, and from a scrimmage in the mouth of the goal, Pierce kicked the fifth goal for the home team. J. E. Davies by a brilliant shot when near the posts, added the sixth goal, and Bryan kicked the seventh. The game was now completely in the hands of the home players, and before the call of time three more goals were added to the already high score, thus ending the game with ten goals to none for the home team. Bryan, Roach, J. E. Davies, J. Davies, figured well for the victors, and Southworth, Higginson, McMillan and Lockwood played a good game for the visitors. The teams were as follows :—Oswestry : Goal, R. O. Davies ; backs, S. Powell (capt.) and Isaac Jones ; half-backs, J. Pierce. M. Evans and T. Ellis ; right wing, J. E. Davies and W. Williams ; left wing, T. Bryan and J. Roach ; centre, J. Davies. Chester : Goal, G. James ; backs, Southworth and Higginson ; half-backs, Hack, Roberts and A. Evans (sub.) ; right wing, J. B. McMillan and Lockwood ; left wing, Banks and Groves (sub.) ; centre, H. Clare. Umpires, Messrs. W. H. Gough and W. Wilkes. Referee, Mr. W. T. Foulkes.

Chester played their first fixture at Earlestown on 5 September 1885. The result was not recorded in the Chester newspapers of the day, although later accounts suggest that the game was lost. The first match to be reported locally was their second game, a 10-0 defeat at Oswestry, two weeks later. Perhaps some excuse for this crushing defeat can be found in the fact that Oswestry, beaten Welsh Cup finalists the previous season, fielded five Welsh internationals. Indeed, referee Bill Foulkes was also an Oswestry player and Welsh international. One of the internationals in the team, the strongly-built full-back and captain Seth Powell, went on to play for Chester in 1892 after a professional career with West Bromwich Albion and Burton Swifts. It is interesting to note that the *Chronicle* reporter uses the name Chester City, although this title was not officially adopted until 1983.

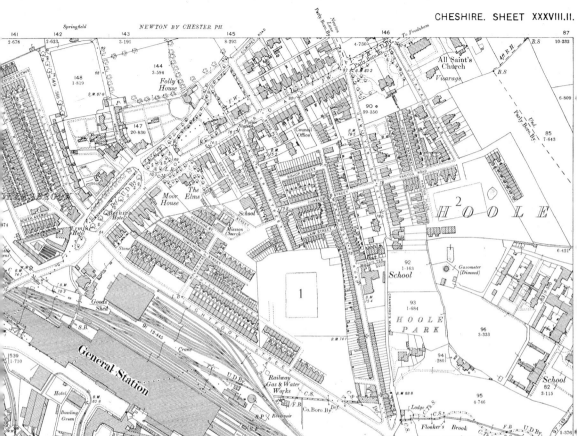

The Ordinance Survey map of Hoole in 1899 shows the two grounds used by the club before the turn of the century. Chester Rovers first played at Faulkner Street (1) in 1884 and the ground was adopted by Chester on their formation in 1885. The first fixture played by the club at Faulkner Street was a 0-3 defeat by Northwich Victoria on 26 September 1885, where a reported attendance of around 750 paid total gate receipts of £16 0s 10d. In the early years, the dressing rooms were located at the Ermine Hotel and access to the ground was along the side of the Beehive Hotel – which initially lead to an area of open fields. During the 1890s, Hoole expanded rapidly and houses were built on the area now covered by Walker Street, Tomkinson Street, Phillip Street and Pickering Street. At this point it became possible to access the ground down Tomkinson Street and this name was often used as an alternative to Faulkner Street. The fairly basic ground was initially no more than a field surrounded by rope, with a modest stand accommodating about fifty supporters. In March 1888, a concert was held at the Royalty Theatre on behalf of the club, which raised £15 and contributed towards the building of a sixty-six-yard grandstand. The pitch itself left a great deal to be desired, containing large furrows which filled with water after heavy rain. In 1898, the encroaching building work forced a relocation to the Enclosed Ground in Hoole (2), also known as the Old Showground, where the Royal Agricultural Show had been held in 1893. The stay here proved brief as new housing forced the club to vacate the ground after only one season and the club was forced to disband for two seasons while a new home was found.

Chester players pose with their first piece of silverware, the Yerburgh Cup, which they won by defeating Northwich Victoria 5-0 in the Chester Charity Cup final in May 1890. From left to right, back row: T. Fleming, F. Lee, R. Roberts, E. McCarthy, G. Dickson, S. Jones, T. McCarthy, R. Davies. Middle row: Wray (secretary), Paris (chairman). Front row: C. Lowe, A. Turner, B. Lewis. Sam Jones became the first Chester player to win international honours when he played for Wales against Scotland in March 1890 while Arthur Turner had become the club's first registered professional, in 1886, after being bought out of the army for £25.

Ben Lewis joined Chester in 1888 and won his first international cap for Wales, against Ireland, in February 1891. An 'effective passer' who possessed 'admirable judgement and a well-directed shot', Lewis went on to win a further 9 caps with Wrexham and Middlesbrough. He returned to Chester in September 1895, but stayed only one season before re-joining Combination rivals Wrexham. He finished his playing career with Buckley Victoria.

Billy Lewis (no relation to Ben) was Chester's most capped player until Angus Eve in 2000. Lewis, pictured here in his Welsh international kit, was described as a speedy and clever forward and represented Wales on 13 occasions while playing for Chester. Born in Bangor, in 1864, he had the honour of playing for Everton in their first ever Football League match and also played League football for Crewe Alexandra and Manchester City. Although predominantly a centre forward, Lewis played in a variety of positions for Chester and even played in goal in one Combination fixture against Wrexham in 1897. He was later a publican at the Duke of York pub in Chester and died in 1935.

Bert Lipsham was the first of four members of the Lipsham family to play for the club, making his first appearance in 1896. After just over a season at Chester, he signed for Crewe Alexandra, followed by First Division Sheffield United in 1898. While playing for the Yorkshire club he played in two FA Cup finals and was capped for England, against Wales, in 1902. In 1904 he moved to Fulham and then Millwall, where he became the club's first manager in 1911. He later coached West Norwood and managed Northfleet. In 1923, Lipsham emigrated to Canada, where he tragically lost his right hand in a timber-yard accident in Toronto and died in a train crash in 1932.

The Chester team with the Cheshire Senior Cup in 1897, which they won for the second time after defeating Northwich Victoria 2-1 at Macclesfield. From left to right, back row: G. Barnes, F. Porter, Dr Butt, W. Coventry, T. Clarke. Middle row: T. Blakeman, A. Catherall, W. Carter. Front row: T. Gordon, C. Spencer, W. Lewis, J. Speakman, J. Lipsham.

Jack Lipsham was a highly respected and admired outside left, who played his first game for Chester in 1903 and his final game in 1921. This eighteen-year run was only interrupted by a short spell at Liverpool in 1906/07, where he made 3 First Division appearances, and a season at Wrexham in 1913/14. Although only 5ft 6in tall, he was a well-built player and his speed down the wing and accurate crosses meant that he was often closely marked by two players during games. He won a Welsh Cup winner's medal with Chester in 1908 and was a member of the team that won the Combination League in 1909. Lipsham was also an enthusiastic cricketer and was captain of St John's Cricket Club. He later became general manager of the Chester Steam Laundry in Heath Lane, Boughton.

The Chester team pictured before the first game at Sealand Road, against Bangor, on 15 December 1906. From left to right, back row: B. Eardley (trainer), Mr C.J. Hughes, Mr J.O. Jepson, J. Russell, Mr B.E. Johnson, W. Keeley, Mr J. Dodd, J. Jones, Mr E. Case, Mr W. Fletcher (secretary). Middle row (seated): Mr E.T. Hallmark, R. Jones, F. Grainger, W. Galley, Mr O. Reeves. Front row: H. Williams, A. Lees, W. Walker, W. Jones, Jenkins. Chester won this inaugural game 4-0, with goals from Jenkins, Walker, Williams and Wallace Jones. The club had moved the short distance to Sealand Road after five years at Whipcord Lane and the ground was acquired thanks to the influence of local Liberal MP Alfred Mond, who negotiated a ten-year lease from the Earl of Crewe, the owner of the land. The ground was built at a cost of only £725 but was incomplete for the Bangor game and it was January 1907 before the covered accommodation was completed. The new ground was a vast improvement on Whipcord Lane, where Chester had played since 1901. The small dimensions of the previous ground had effectively barred Chester from the FA Cup, and its location – close to a stream – meant that the pitch resembled a swamp for much of the season. Chester were virtually impregnable at the new Sealand Road enclosure, and their home League record in the first six years at the ground read: Played 86, Won 74, Drawn 9, Lost 3, Goals For 293, Goals Against 82. An impressive record by anyone's standards.

GRAND FOOTBALL MATCH,

SATURDAY, OCT. 12TH, 1907,

CHESTER v. BIRKENHEAD.

CHESTER.

GOAL.

Dodd.

BACKS.

Right.   Left.

Russell.   Grundy.

HALF-BACKS.

Right.   Centre.   Left.

Matthews.   Grainger.   Gordon (Capt.)

FORWARDS.

Right Wing.   Centre.   Left Wing.

Williams.   Lees.   Freeman.   Jones.   Lipsham.

O

Norris.   Molyneux.   Morgan.   Stewart.   Williams.

Left Wing   Centre.   Right Wing.

FORWARDS.

Richards.   Hancock.   Headon.

Left.   Centre.   Right.

HALF-BACKS.

London.   Bantom.

Left.   Right.

BACKS.

Chapman.

GOAL.

BIRKENHEAD.

Chester first produced an official programme for games in the 1907/08 season and this one, against Birkenhead, is numbered as issue three. The folded pink sheet, slightly larger than A4, was printed by Taplen and Paddock of Eastgate Row and contained a surprising amount of reading on the reverse side of the line-ups. The printer, Josiah Taplen, went on to become chairman of the football club between 1920 and 1928. Chester won this game 8-0, with hat-tricks from Wallace Jones and Joe Freeman and single strikes from Jack Lipsham and Horace Williams.

The 1907/08 season proved to be the most successful campaign for the club so far and the players and directors can be seen with the Cheshire Senior Cup (left) and Welsh Cup. From left to right, back row: Mr E. Webster, Mr B.E. Johnson, Councillor J. Dodd, Mr L. Davies, Mr W. Wildgoose, Mr O. Reeves. Standing: Mr O. Jepson, J. Russell, Mr W. Fletcher (secretary), W. Keeley, Mr E.T. Hallmark, J. Grundy, Mr L. Hales. Sitting: B. Eardley (trainer) W. Matthews, F. Grainger, T. Gordon (captain), A. Appleton. Front row: H. Williams, A. Lees, J. Freeman, W. Jones, B. Goode, J. Lipsham. Chester won the Welsh Cup for the first time after defeating Connah's Quay United 3-1, in front of 8,000 spectators at Wrexham, with goals from Bert Goode (2) and Arthur Lees. The team that won the trophy was: Keeley, Wightman, Russell, Matthews, Grainger, Gordon, Williams, Lees, Freeman, Goode, Lipsham. The Cheshire Senior Cup was secured for the fourth time after a 4-2 victory over Altrincham at Crewe. The club also finished as runners-up in the Combination for the fifth successive season. On this occasion they lost out, on goal average, to Tranmere Rovers. One of the most popular players at the time was Billy Matthews, who had joined the club in 1903 and remained with Chester until the outbreak of war, apart from a short spell with Rhyl in 1906 and 1907. Predominantly a half-back, Matthews was capped for Wales, against Ireland, in 1905 and was a member of the Welsh team defeated 7-1 by England in 1908. Contemporary programmes described him as 'one of the most brilliant and consistent players the club has ever possessed'. He joined up at the outbreak of war, but suffered during the hostilities, and died in 1921 at the early age of thirty-eight.

In 1908/09, Chester finally secured the Combination title, finishing eight points clear of Saltney. They also retained the Cheshire Senior Cup with a 3-0 victory over Northwich Victoria at Crewe. This is the team that faced Wrexham Reserves in March 1909. From left to right, back row (players only): Bentley, Russell, Keeley, Davies, Gordon. Front row: Stockton, Roberts, Freeman, Grainger, Lappin, Lipsham.

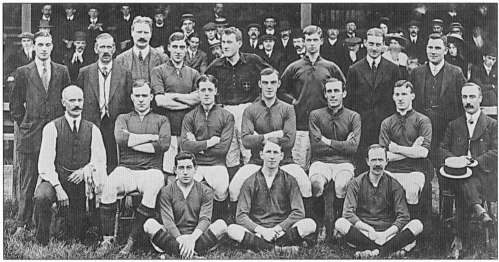

By 1910, the directors had become concerned about the standard of football offered by the Combination and an application to join the Lancashire Combination was accepted. The supporters clearly felt the same way, as attendances had dropped for the first time since the re-formation of the club and a heavy financial loss had been reported. This was the team that represented the club in their first game in the Lancashire Combination. From left to right, back row: S. Dorset, E.T. Hallmark (director), A.E. Jones (director), F. Simpson, G. Bancroft, H. Wright, L. Davies (director), O. Reeves (director). Middle row: D. Slyfield (trainer), J. Yuill, W. Smith, J. Blackburn, B. Chetwood, J. Lipsham, W. Fletcher (secretary). Front row: W. Matthews, E. Tremlett, T. Gordon.

An unusual programme was issued by Chester for their Welsh Cup second round tie against local rivals the 'Chainboys' of Saltney in December 1911. Taplen and Paddock's programme 'issued under the auspices of Chester Football Club' was unusual in that the game was actually a home tie for Saltney and the match was played at their Mount Pleasant Ground. The Saltney enclosure clearly did not meet the standards of Chester's pitch as 'Bevys', who wrote the club gossip section in the programme, described how 'Visitors need to be wary of the pranks played by the ball around the diminutive mounds and miniature valleys which abound'. The game finished 1-1, but Chester convincingly won the replay 4-1 at Sealand Road and went on to reach the semi-final, where they were defeated by Cardiff City.

Chester's published accounts for the 1921/22 season revealed that the club made a loss of £460 5s 5d over the season (the incorrect figure had been printed in the report and amended to match the profit and loss account inside). As the report reveals, the biggest drain on resources were the players' wages (£2,133 17s 0d) and Entertainment Tax (£1,176 17s 4d). This all came out of gate receipts, which totalled £4,645 18s 7d for the season. The accounts reveal that no money was received from transfers, but £30 was paid in transfer fees to bring players into the club. The large loss helped sway the club away from making an application to join the recently formed Third Division (North), as they feared a large increase in travel expenses would put further pressure on already strained financial resources.

19

In 1921/22, Chester won the Cheshire County League for the first time, as well as the Hospital Charity competition – for which they were awarded the Sir Owen Phillips Cup. Chester had been one of the founder members of the league in 1919 and they had secured the title in style with nine successive victories at the end of the season. From left to right, back row: T. Brown (trainer), W.H. Ebrey (director), G.H. Russell (director), J. Taplen (chairman), J. Blaylock (director), H. Gray (director), B. Walton (director), H. Dunning (director). Middle row: R.O. Berry (secretary), W.A. Wood (director), H. Percival, S. Ashcroft, J. Pugh, J.W. Pryde, F.J. Quinn (director), H. Mansley (director). Sitting: C. Spencer (trainer), H.B. Howarth, Trevor Jones, J. Donnachie (captain), W. Robinson (vice-captain), Tom Jones, C.E. Jones, J. Ronson. Front row: T. Pimlott, A.E. Virr. The schoolboy, holding the ball, is Joe Donnachie's son. Donnachie himself was a former Scottish international, who had also played for Oldham Athletic, Everton, Blackpool and Glasgow Rangers. After retiring from the game, he was the publican at the Mariner's Arms in New Crane Street.

This nine-carat gold medal was awarded to Joe Donnachie after Chester's 3-0 victory against Buckley in the Hospital Charity Cup. The competition was staged annually in the early 1920s to raise money for Chester Royal Infirmary. The final itself was played in the middle of May, in weather rather more suited to cricket than football, and was not without controversy. Pimlott and Virr scored for Chester, before Emlyn Jones was sent off for Buckley. Crofts, the Buckley captain, resented the decision and made to leave the pitch, but was persuaded to turn back by Chester's Trevor Jones. Virr added a third for Chester as Buckley finished the game with nine men, following an injury to another of their players.

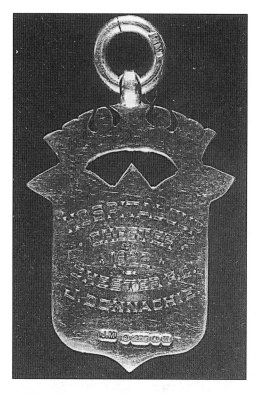

New Brighton's Lyon heads the ball past Chester goalkeeper Ashcroft at Sandheys Park in the 1922 FA Cup preliminary qualifying round. The Rakers won the game 4-2 in front of 9,000 spectators, with Chester's goals coming from Howarth and Gittens.

Chester players line up in traditional 2-3-5 formation before the FA Cup game against Ellesmere Port Cement in September 1923. Chester won the game 1-0. From left to right, back row: C. Spencer (trainer), Stroud, J. Pugh, R. Simpson. Middle row: Garrett, W. Heath, C. Williams. Front row: H. Howarth, T. Parton, J. McGivney, Dempsey, Partington.

CHESTER FOOTBALL CLUB, LTD.

Secretary:
B. G. DICKIN,
73, Catherine St.,
CHESTER.

Tel. 706.

Dec 4th 1923

Dear Sir,

Please note that you have been selected to play for Chester against Ellesmere Port *, on* Sat Dec 8th *at* E. Port *.* ~~Train~~ Chara *leaves* Chester General *Station at* 1-30 *.* **Kick-off** 2-30 **p.m.** *Notify me at once if you cannot play.*

LOST 2-0

Yours truly,

B. G. DICKIN, Secretary.

This postcard was sent to full-back Jack Mack to notify him of his selection for Chester's reserve team fixture, in the West Cheshire League, at Ellesmere Port. Chester lost the game 2-0, a big turn-around from the previous week when Chester had beaten the same team 12-1 at Sealand Road.

Chester claimed their second Cheshire County League championship in 1925/26, after a 2-2 draw with Ashton National. The event was marked by this cartoon in the *Chester Chronicle*. The Chester side contained a number of experienced players, including full-backs Jack Barton and Tweedle Rigg who had played together at Rochdale. In the centre of defence, former Third Lanark and Sunderland defender Archie Jackson was the hero of the fans, while the forward line included leading scorers Harold Peters and George Parkin (both ex-Southport) and Peter Rothwell (formerly of Tranmere Rovers).

The players pose proudly with the Cheshire County League trophy after securing the 1925/26 title with a record number of points.

Charlie Hewitt was appointed secretary-manager of Chester in 1930, after impressing the board of directors with his work at Connah's Quay and Shotton – where he had won the Welsh Cup in 1929 and guided them to the runners-up position in the Cheshire County League in 1930. Chairman Harry Mansley gave Hewitt a free hand to do everything in his power to bring League football to the city. Within a few weeks, Hewitt had totally transformed the club by bringing in experienced Football League players, who were 'available for transfer' at their respective clubs, and financing these imports by increasing ticket prices. The bold tactics paid dividends and supporters flocked to the ground to watch players of the calibre of Scottish international Dave Morris, Frank Cresswell, Arthur Gale and Paddy Clifford.

25

CHESTER v. CARDIFF CITY.

Welsh Senior Cup.

Wednesday, March 25th 1931, Kick-off 5-15 p.m.

Changes in Teams will be announced.

CHESTER

Right   Left

Jarvie

Bennett   McCloy

Atkinson   Morris   Neale

Clifford   Irvine   Gale   Cresswell   Dickie

O

McGarth   Jones   McCambridge   Merry   Emmerson

Blackburn   Galraith or Keenor   Harris

Roberts   Smith or Hardy

Farquharson

Left   Right

CARDIFF CITY

The line-ups in the programme for the Welsh Cup sixth round tie against Cardiff City. A record attendance of 11,507 saw the Second Division side narrowly defeat Chester by a single goal. Within ten days the attendance record had been broken, when 13,150 were present for the opening of the new stand extension prior to the crucial league game against Port Vale Reserves.

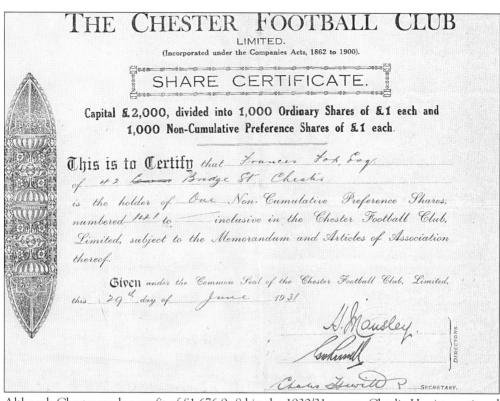

THE CHESTER FOOTBALL CLUB
LIMITED.
(Incorporated under the Companies Acts, 1862 to 1900).

SHARE CERTIFICATE.

Capital £2,000, divided into 1,000 Ordinary Shares of £1 each and 1,000 Non-Cumulative Preference Shares of £1 each.

This is to Certify that *Frances Fox, Esq.* of *42 Lower Bridge St Chester* is the holder of *One* Non-Cumulative Preference *Shares,* numbered *141 to* inclusive in the *Chester Football Club, Limited,* subject to the Memorandum and Articles of Association thereof.

Given under the Common Seal of the Chester Football Club, Limited, this *29th* day of *June* *1931*.

H. Mausley.

DIRECTORS.

Charles Hewitt SECRETARY.

Although Chester made a profit of £1,676 9s 8d in the 1930/31 season, Charlie Hewitt continued to emphasise the importance of raising finance for the club. At the end of May 1931, a scheme was launched at the Town Hall in order to raise an extra £1,000 for the club by doubling the share capital. This share certificate was issued to Francis Fox for a single £1 non-cumulative preference share. The money raised was spent on new players and ground improvements.

Chester's successful 1930/31 season owed a great deal to the phenomenal goalscoring exploits of Arthur Gale. The Salford schoolmaster scored an incredible 73 goals in only 39 league games. He also set an individual Chester record by scoring seven goals in the Welsh Cup against Llanfairfechan. Gale briefly returned to Sealand Road, from West Bromwich Albion, in 1936, but was unable to re-create the golden touch of the 1930/31 season.

These views of the stadium, taken in the middle of 1931, appeared in Chester's application brochure to the Football League and showed how much the ground had developed during the late 1920s and early '30s. The railings around the ground were replaced by a concrete wall in 1935.

The Sealand Road End was partially covered in 1927 but extended to cover the whole area behind the goal during the 1930/31 season. The barrel roof, supported by sixteen pillars, became known as the Barn and remained *in situ* until 1987, when the badly rusting roof was replaced.

The small stand on the popular side was erected in 1926 and extended in 1934. It was the late 1960s before the side was completely covered.

The central main stand was re-erected after the First World War and opened in December 1920. The wing extension was built at a cost of £1,000 and opened before the game against Port Vale Reserves in April 1931. Within three months the stand had been extended to cover the complete length of the ground. Admission cost 2s 4d for the centre stand and 1s 6d for the wing stands.

Chester players and directors with the Cheshire Senior Cup in 1931, prior to the club's election to the Football League. On the back row, the directors flank Charlie Hewitt (fifth from left). From left to right, middle row: -?-, -?-, -?-, Dave Morris, Phil McCloy, Harry Mansley (chairman), Johnnie Jarvie, Fred Bennett, Fred Burgess, Tommy Neale, Jock Simpson (trainer). Front row: Joshua Atkinson, Paddy Clifford, Bobby Irvine, Arthur Gale, Frank Cresswell, Jimmy Dickie, -?-. Despite scoring 170 goals, Chester were only able to finish as runners-up to Port Vale Reserves in the Cheshire County League. On 1 June 1931, Chester were elected to the Football League on a second ballot after the initial vote had produced a tie. Chester's election surprised many people, after all the club's previous attempts, in 1928 and 1929, had produced no support whatsoever. However, in 1931 the board of directors had a different story to tell. Attendances had soared during 1930/31 and the club had made a profit of £1,600 as enthusiasm reached unprecedented levels. In addition, the ground had been developed to produce a neat enclosure culminating in a grandstand, now nearing completion, which held 4,500. The opening of the first wing of the stand, for the Good Friday match against Port Vale Reserves, had taken place in the presence of Charles Sutcliffe, president of the Football League, and Alderman Cropper, the chairman of Chesterfield and the Third Division (North). The two influential gentleman were reportedly very impressed by the facilities offered by Chester, and there is little doubt that the favourable impression created by the club that day went a long way to securing support.

Two
The 1930s and the War Years
1931-1946

Chester players prepare for their first game in the Football League. In the background, workmen complete work on the extension to the main stand which brought the seating capacity up to 4,500.

Chester's programme for their first season in the Football League was an eight-page folded effort, containing very little reading matter but over forty advertisements. Prominent among the advertisers were the Saltney company J. Crichton, who had constructed the extensions to the main stand. The game itself, against Gateshead, finished as a 1-1 draw, Chester's goal being scored by Cyril Matthews in front of 10,195 spectators.

Baden Herod, Harry Skitt and Tommy Jennings were three of the players signed by Charlie Hewitt for the first season in the Football League. Herod and Skitt cost a total of £500 from Tottenham, while Jennings, a prolific scorer with Leeds United, was appointed captain.

In January 1933, Chester achieved an outstanding 5-0 victory over Second Division Fulham in the FA Cup third round, with four of the goals coming from outside left Foster Hedley and one from Arthur Mercer. A crowd of 14,328 paid £948 in gate receipts. The ticket shows that supporters had to pay 3s 6d for the best seats in the centre stand. The Fulham victory put Chester in the fourth round for the first time in their history, where they were favourites to overcome struggling divisional rivals Halifax Town. Unfortunately, a goal-less draw at a frost-bound Sealand Road was followed by a narrow 3-2 defeat in Yorkshire.

CHESTER F.C., LTD.

Chester v. Fulham

14th Jan., 1933
Kick-off 2-30 p.m.
Block B
Row C

No. **123**

GRAND STAND, Centre
PRICE 3/6
(including tax)

This portion to be retained and produced to Steward before occupying a seat.

Chas. Hewitt, Sec-Man

31

Both John Wallbanks and goalkeeper Bob Middleton joined Chester in the early months of 1934. Wallbanks joined the club from Portsmouth while Middleton, a former Scottish international custodian, had been registered with Sunderland. Middleton was later host at the Customs House Inn in Watergate Street.

This Chester team started the 1934/35 season with four successive victories. From left to right, back row: Fred Bennett, Johnnie Pitcairn, Bob Middleton, Arthur Wilson, Ernie 'Henry' Hall, John Fantham, Hughie Ross (trainer). Front row: Jackie Hughes, Ernie Whittam, John Wallbanks, Frank Cresswell, Charlie Sargeant.

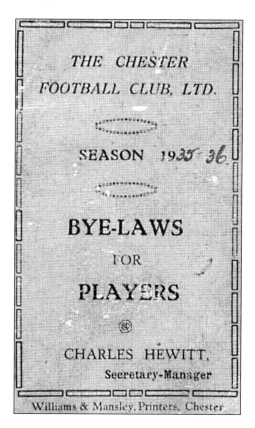

There were strict regulations for the players during Charlie Hewitt's reign as secretary-manager as this booklet, issued to Bill Horsman in 1935, reveals. Rule 1 laid down the training times for the players, who were expected to report to the dressing rooms at 10 a.m. and 2 p.m. on Tuesday, Wednesday, Thursday and Friday each week. To confirm their attendance, all the players had to sign the trainer's record-of-attendance book every morning and afternoon, as laid down in rule 19.

3.—All Players and Reserves must be on the ground three-quarters of an hour before the kick-off for home matches and at the Station 15 minutes before the train starts for away matches. Any player who is chosen to play in any match, or elected on reserve, can only be excused from playing by producing on the day preceding, or morning of the match, a certificate from the Medical Adviser of the Club. Except under special circumstances players will not be written to either as to Training, playing in Matches, Times of Kick-off, Trains, etc. Each Player must take notice from the the list of instructions as posted in the Dressing Room every Thursday afternoon, and if any player shall fail to play in any match for which he is selected as one of the Team, he shall forfeit one week's wages and be further dealt with as the Directors may determine.

4.—Bags are provided for the use of the player's outfit to away matches, and each player will be held responsible for loss of either.

5.—Players are expected to be most careful in their use of language on the field of play, in the dressing and players' rooms, and whilst travelling to and from away matches.

6.—Any case of illness or accident must be reported to the Manager or Trainer immediately,

7.—Smoking is strictly prohibited in the Dressing Rooms, and also in the Saloons on the day of the Match.

8.—No player to absent himself from any duties without first obtaining the sanction of the Manager; and all players not selected for any match must be present on the ground.

9.—Players must not bring friends into the ground or dressing rooms either on training or match days

10.—No Player shall be allowed to bet on any match. Any player breaking this rule shall be suspended till the case can be investigated by the Directors.

11.—The Captains of the Teams shall have full control on the the field of play and the Players shall readily accept their orders.

12.—Any Player or Players having a grievance at any time must lay the same before the Manager, who will report to the Directors.

13.—Any Player wanting to stay over the week-end in any town must make application to the Manager before the Directors' meeting.

14.—No one will be allowed in the Dressing Room excepting Players and Officials of the Club, either before or after matches and during training hours.

15 —Players are not to enter Licensed premises or attend Whist Drives and Dances after Wednesday in each week, without first obtaining the permission of the Directors or Secretary-Manager.

John Wallbanks scores Chester's opening goal in the 4-0 victory over Accrington Stanley on 1 September 1934. Wallbanks was transferred to Bradford Park Avenue in March 1935, after scoring an impressive 36 goals in only 38 appearances. Chester themselves finished third in the Third Division (North) in 1934/35, three points behind champions Doncaster Rovers. The also reached the third round of the FA Cup and the final of the Welsh Cup, where they were beaten by Tranmere Rovers.

Arthur Wilson is given the responsibility of looking after the Third Division (North) Cup, after the players and directors arrive at Chester General Station from Darlington in April 1936.

Charlie Sargeant, Arthur Wilson and Bill Horsman parade the Third Division (North) Cup along Eastgate Street in April 1936. Chester won the trophy after defeating Darlington 2-1, with goals from Horsman and Frank Wrightson. Three days after this victory, Chester were beaten by Crewe in the Welsh Cup final. For both these matches, chairman Harry Mansley was in temporary charge of the team as Charlie Hewitt had resigned as manager on 1 April to take up a similar position at Millwall. The Chester team that won the cup was: Burke, Common, Hall, Pitcairn, Wilson, Howarth, Horsman, Wharton, Wrightson, Sanders, Sargeant. The following season, Chester retained the trophy by defeating Southport 3-1 at Haig Avenue. Charlie Sargeant, who joined Chester in March 1934 from Hull City, played in both of these finals. An outside left, with excellent speed and a telling shot, Sargeant was a temperamental player who always tried hard, but was often the subject of criticism by supporters. He was once reputed to have confronted a critic in the main stand in the middle of a game.

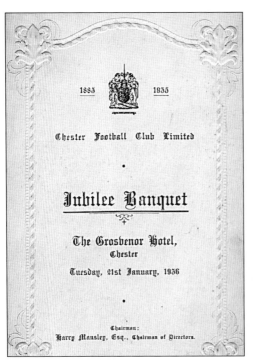

1885 1935

Chester Football Club Limited

•

Jubilee Banquet

The Grosvenor Hotel,
Chester

Tuesday, 21st January, 1936

•

Chairman:
Harry Mansley, Esq., Chairman of Directors.

Chester celebrated their Golden Jubilee in 1935. The club had initially prepared for the event in 1933, before realising they were two years too early. In the event, the banquet had to be postponed on 21 January 1936, following the death of King George V the previous day.

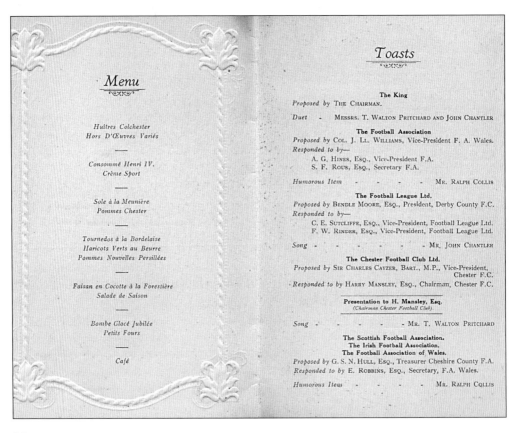

Menu

Huîtres Colchester
Hors D'Œuvres Variés

———

Consommé Henri IV.
Crème Sport

———

Sole à la Meunière
Pommes Chester

———

Tournedos à la Bordelaise
Haricots Verts au Beurre
Pommes Nouvelles Persillées

———

Faisan en Cocotte à la Forestière
Salade de Saison

———

Bombe Glacé Jubilée
Petits Fours

———

Café

Toasts

The King
Proposed by THE CHAIRMAN.

Duet   -   MESSRS. T. WALTON PRITCHARD AND JOHN CHANTLER

The Football Association
Proposed by COL. J. LL. WILLIAMS, Vice-President F. A. Wales.
Responded to by—
    A. G. HINES, ESQ., Vice-President F.A.
    S. F. ROUS, ESQ., Secretary F.A.

Humorous Item   -   -   -   MR. RALPH COLLIS

The Football League Ltd.
Proposed by BENDLE MOORE, ESQ., President, Derby County F.C.
Responded to by—
    C. E. SUTCLIFFE, ESQ., Vice-President, Football League Ltd.
    F. W. RINDER, ESQ., Vice-President, Football League Ltd.

Song   -   -   -   -   -   MR. JOHN CHANTLER

The Chester Football Club Ltd.
Proposed by SIR CHARLES CAYZER, BART., M.P., Vice-President, Chester F.C.
Responded to by HARRY MANSLEY, ESQ., Chairman, Chester F.C.

Presentation to H. Mansley, Esq.
(Chairman Chester Football Club)

Song   -   -   -   -   -   MR. T. WALTON PRITCHARD

The Scottish Football Association.
The Irish Football Association.
The Football Association of Wales.
Proposed by G. S. N. HULL, ESQ., Treasurer Cheshire County F.A.
Responded to by E. ROBBINS, ESQ., Secretary, F.A. Wales.

Humorous Item   -   -   -   MR. RALPH COLLIS

A solid defensive header from Arthur Wilson. 'Tug' Wilson joined Chester, as an inside left, from West Ham United for £275, but was successfully converted to centre half by Charlie Hewitt. He made 136 League appearances before joining Wolves in 1937.

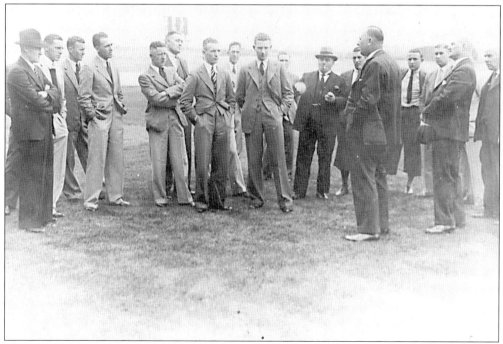

Chairman Harry Mansley addresses the players in 1936, following the appointment of Alex Raisbeck (second from right) as manager. Mansley was chairman from 1928 to 1938.

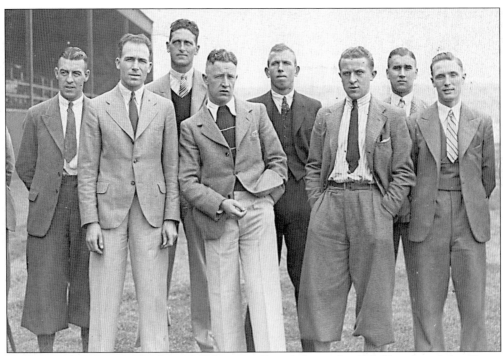

Well-dressed newcomers for the 1936/37 season. From left to right: Bill Chambers, John Gurry, Bert Gray, Stan Prout, Tom Alderson, John Turner, 'Bos' Trevis, Peter Percival.

Golf has always been a popular pastime for footballers. Here, Arthur Wilson and Bill Chambers admire Bill Horsman's stance at Upton-by-Chester Golf Club.

Players, directors and staff assemble in front of the main stand in 1937. From left to right, back row: A. Raisbeck (manager), H. Mansley (chairman), W.T. Rowley , A. Harrison, H. Paddock, G.H. Russell, R.A. Houdley (reporter), A. Wilson, A. Gray, F. Cresswell, E. Hall, A. Trevis, E.J. Lidbury, Dr W. Hughes, C. Farr, W. Turner (vice-chairman), Mr Hughes (senior), K. Crispin (hon. solicitor), E. Partin. Middle row: Beaumont (assistant trainer), F. Wrightson, C. Sargeant, T. Alderson, R. Done, W. Peters (secretary), R. Sanders, E. Common, Master Argyle, S. Argyle. Front row: J. Collins (trainer), T. Walters, T. Feeney, C. Smith, J. McCreary, P. McCarthy, W. Horsman. Ralph Houdley (or RAH as he was known) was the football reporter for the *Cheshire Observer* from 1926 through to the early 1970s.

Full-back Ted Common joined Chester at the end of July 1935 from Preston North End, having previously played for New Delavel, Blyth Spartans and Everton, where he made 14 League appearances. A great club man, Common was an excellent tackler and positional player with a powerful kick, who was regarded as one of the best defenders in the Northern Section. He made 142 appearances for Chester between 1935 and 1939, and was ever present in the 1936/37 season.

In May 1938, Frank Brown (right) resigned as Torquay United manager and succeeded Alex Raisbeck at Chester. Brown, a former player with Blackpool and Exeter City, had joined Torquay United in 1923, where he had taken over as trainer on retirement from playing. He had helped Torquay establish themselves as a Football League side, becoming manager in May 1932. He remained as manager of Chester until May 1953. Septimus Atterbury, a former player with Leicester Fosse, Barnsley, Swindon Town and Plymouth Argyle, was appointed trainer – a position he had previously held at Argyle for sixteen years.

There were seven newcomers to the Chester team in 1938/39. From left to right, back row: Joe McGough, Bill Pendergast, Chris Robertson, Arthur Keeley. Front row: Cliff Owen, Albert Ross, Joe Rogers. Pendergast went on to create a Chester record by scoring in 13 successive games between 10 September and 3 December 1938. He was unlucky not to extend this record to 14 after Chester were awarded a penalty in the FA Cup against Hull City. Pendergast wanted to take the spot-kick himself but, with Chester trailing 2-1, he was overruled by captain Willis Gregg who took the responsibility himself and scored.

Joe McGough and Bill Horsman in pre-season training. McGough joined the club from Reading in 1938 and went on to become a member of the coaching staff in the 1950s. Horsman moved to Chester from Birmingham in 1935 and made 141 appearances before the outbreak of war.

This cartoon appeared in the local papers following a 2-2 draw with Hull City in the second round of the FA Cup. Chester won the replay 1-0. After victory over Coventry City in the third round, they went on to meet Sheffield Wednesday in the last thirty-two, but were eventually beaten 2-0 after two drawn games. The first replay, at Sealand Road, drew a record attendance of 18,816.

Goalkeeper Alf Hobson joined Chester from Liverpool in October 1938. The £700 fee was a record for the club at the time. Hobson had a shaky start in Chester colours and conceded thirteen goals in his first four games. After losing his place in February 1939, he regained the goalkeeping shirt for the final seventeen games of the season. He retained the position at the start of 1939/40 and played in the first three games before the outbreak of war brought an abrupt end to League football.

Manager Frank Brown explains the latest team formations to his players in the late 1930s.

A 1d single-sheet programme was available for this match at Everton, which not only counted for the Lancashire Cup but also the Wartime League North championship. Chester lost the game 4-1. Wartime football gave Chester the opportunity to play opponents they would not normally face, such as Everton, Liverpool and Manchester United. During the war, clubs relied on the use of guest players, who were often stationed at Army bases nearby. Two of the most famous names to play for Chester were England international Joe Mercer and Arsenal full-back Leslie Compton. For the Everton game, Chester included Scottish international Andy Black from Hearts, who was a regular guest throughout the war.

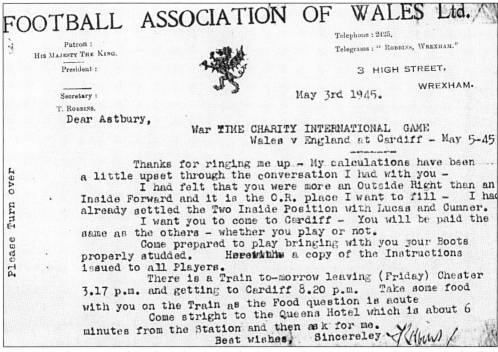

Tommy Astbury was selected to play for Wales in a wartime international against England in 1945 although, as this letter shows, there seemed to be some doubt about what position he would play. In the event, he wore the unfamiliar number 7 shirt.

Goalkeeper Bill Shortt signed for Chester before the war and made more than 100 wartime appearances for the club. In 1946, he joined Plymouth Argyle for £1,000 and went on to play for Wales on 12 occasions. He returned to Chester in January 1947 to play for Argyle against Chester in an FA Cup third round tie. On that day, former colleagues Tommy Astbury and Tommy Burden put two goals past him as Ches won 2-0.

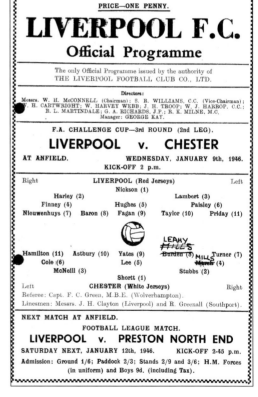

The 1945/46 season marked the return of FA Cup football, with games played on a two-leg basis for the only time in the history of the tournament. Chester were already 2-0 down from the first leg when they played at Anfield. This flimsy team-sheet was available for the 11,000 spectators who watched Liverpool win 2-1.

Three
After the War
1946-1958

Chester supporters gather outside the Carlton Tavern in Handbridge for an away game at Halifax in December 1946. In the centre of the front row is Mickey Moran, club mascot throughout the 1930s and '40s. In the top left of the picture, wearing a hat, is local man Jimmy Walsh, who was light-heavyweight boxing champion of Britain in the 1930s.

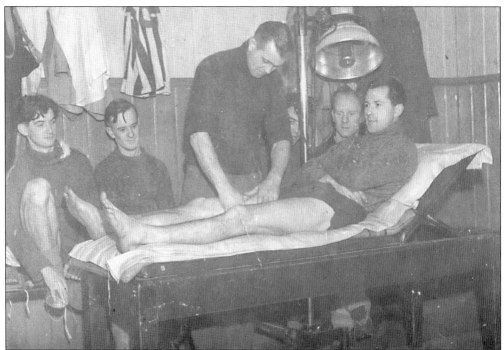

Dick Yates receives treatment prior to the League game against Tranmere in January 1947. Yates scored 36 goals in 40 League games in 1946/47, a record for a Chester player in the Football League. The following season, Yates found the goals harder to come by and, after just a single strike in 12 games, was surprisingly allowed to join Wrexham – where he promptly scored a hat-trick on his debut.

Chester players prepared for the FA Cup fourth round game against Stoke City by retiring to Abergele for a week of special training. As usual, a round of golf was high on the agenda. The game itself attracted huge interest in the city and Chester played above themselves to hold their illustrious opponents, including Stanley Matthews, to a goal-less draw. In the replay, at Stoke, Chester were narrowly defeated 3-2.

Frank Brown lines up alongside Ray Westwood, Chester's major signing from Bolton Wanderers, in December 1947. Westwood had made 6 pre-war international appearances for England and was a major outlay at £2,400. He suffered a series of injuries at Chester and, after scoring 13 goals in 38 appearances, refused to accept terms for the 1949/50 season and left the club. At the time, it was calculated that, after taking wages into consideration, Westwood cost the club £70 every time he played – a sum Chester could ill-afford.

Training on the Annexe, behind the main stand, in readiness for an FA Cup game against Crystal Palace at the start of 1948. In the dark tracksuits are long-serving centre half Trevor Walters and full-back Dave McNeil, who had both signed for the club before the war. Trevor Walters made 151 appearances between 1937 and 1948, while Dave McNeil went on to make 114 appearances.

A spot of head tennis for George Williamson, Tommy Best and Tommy Astbury prior to the Crystal Palace cup tie. Inside forward Best was the first coloured player to play League football for the club and scored on his debut, against Oldham Athletic, in August 1947. In October 1948, he returned to his native South Wales to play for Cardiff City, after scoring 14 goals in 40 games. Best went on to play for Queens Park Rangers, Hereford United and Bromsgrove Rovers. After his retirement from the game, he lived and worked in Hereford.

Eric Lee clears his lines in Chester's 1-0 FA Cup victory at Crystal Palace. The hero of the day was George Scales, who kept the Palace forwards at bay with some magnificent second-half saves.

A Chester line-up from the 1948/49 season. From left to right, back row: Brown (manager), Beaumont, Oliver (trainer), Astbury, Williamson, Scales, McNeil, Butcher, Booth, Mackie. Front row: Davies, Burgess, Harrigan, Foulds, Forsyth.

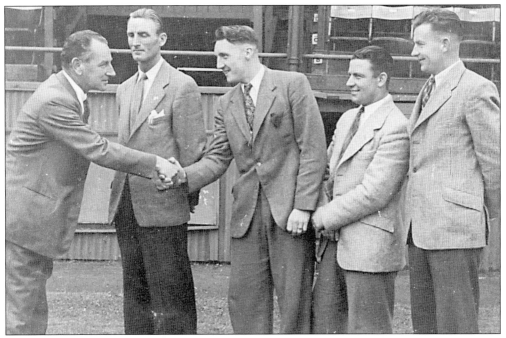

Chairman Sir Thomas Brocklebank welcomes the club's new signings for the 1949/50 season. From left to right: Eric Sibley (who was made captain), Frank Hindle, Harry Jackson and Bill Pearson.

Chester face the camera during the 1949/50 season. From left to right, back row: Tommy Astbury, Reg Butcher, Ted Elliott, Bill Lawton, Eric Lee, Frank Hindle. Front row: Billy Foulkes, Geoff Coffin, Harry Jackson, Albert Burgess, Joe Davies.

Harry Jackson, with his arm upraised, signals Chester's second goal in the 4-1 victory over Southport in August 1949. The Chester number 11 is Bill Pearson, while Joe Davies can be seen behind Jackson.

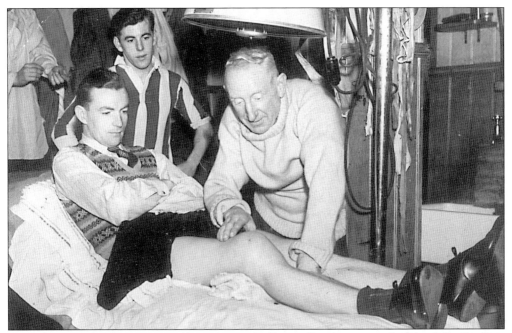

Trainer Jimmy Collins treats Billy Pearson's badly swollen knee, watched by Billy Foulkes. Outside left Pearson joined Chester from Grimsby Town, but found appearances restricted by injury and retired at the end of the 1949/50 season.

Frank Hindle and Ted Elliott take their colleagues for a ride in summer 1950. Players include Hankinson, Lee, Astbury, Morement, Tilston and Burgess.

Wrexham goalkeeper Ferguson gathers the ball under pressure from Albert Burgess in the League game at the Racecourse Ground in September 1950. Burgess scored 54 goals in 111 games before joining Crystal Palace in September 1951.

Billy Foulkes shoots for goal at Wrexham. There were 16,710 spectators present for this match, which Chester lost 2-0.

Tommy Astbury was interviewed by Richard Dimbleby for the British Forces overseas in February 1951. Unfortunately, Chester supporters at home were unable to hear the broadcast, as explained in this letter of thanks from the Head of Broadcasting.

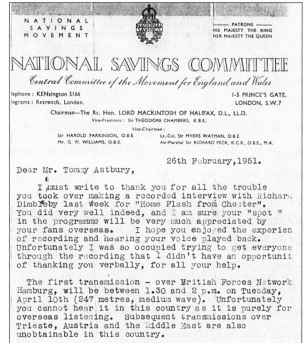

NATIONAL
SAVINGS
MOVEMENT

PATRONS
HIS MAJESTY THE KING
HER MAJESTY THE QUEEN

NATIONAL SAVINGS COMMITTEE
Central Committee of the Movement for England and Wales

lephone : KENsington 5166
legrams : Retrench, London.

1-5 PRINCE'S GATE,
LONDON, S.W.7

Chairman—The Rt. Hon. LORD MACKINTOSH OF HALIFAX, D.L., LL.D.
Vice-President: Sir THEODORE CHAMBERS, K.B.E.

Vice-Chairmen :
Sir HAROLD PARKINSON, O.B.E.   Lt.-Col. Sir MYERS WAYMAN, O.B.E.
Mr. G. H. WILLIAMS, O.B.E.   Air-Marshal Sir RICHARD PECK, K.C.B., O.B.E., M.A.

26th February, 1951.

Dear Mr. Tommy Astbury,

I must write to thank you for all the trouble
you took over making a recorded interview with Richard
Dimbleby last week for "Home Flash from Chester".
You did very well indeed, and I am sure your "spot "
in the programme will be very much appreciated by
your fans overseas.   I hope you enjoyed the experien
of recording and hearing your voice played back.
Unfortunately I was so occupied trying to get everyone
through the recording that I didn't have an opportunit
of thanking you verbally, for all your help.

The first transmission - over British Forces Network
Hamburg, will be between 1.30 and 2 p.m. on Tuesday,
April 10th (247 metres, medium wave). Unfortunately
you cannot hear it in this country as it is purely for
overseas listening. Subsequent transmissions over
Trieste, Austria and the Middle East are also
unobtainable in this country.

With many thanks and best wishes,

Yours sincerely,

Marjorie Goddard

T.Astbury, Esq.,
Sealand Rd., Chester.

HEAD OF BROADCASTING SECTION

Frank Brown welcomes centre forward Bill Jones, a close-season signing from Manchester City, to the Stadium. Also in the picture are the other new arrivals – Comley, Fletcher and Gill – together with chairman Sam Argyle.

Chester line-up for the opening game of the 1951/52 season against Wrexham. From left to right, back row: Ralph Morement, John Molyneux, Harry Threadgold, Eric Lee, Ray Gill, Tommy Astbury. Front row: Billy Foulkes, Bill Jones, Albert Burgess, Joe Hilton, Roger Kirkpatrick.

54

Chairman Sam Argyle and captain Ralph Morement bid farewell to Billy Foulkes at Chester General station. Foulkes was on his way to Newcastle United for a record £12,000. Within a week, Chester had received an additional £500 after the winger won his first international cap for Wales.

Stalwart wing-half Ronnie Hughes signed professional terms with Chester in 1950, but had to wait until 1952 before he made his full League debut, against Rochdale. He went on to play 399 League games for the club before joining Holywell Town in 1962.

A record attendance of 20,358 packed into the ground for the FA Cup replay against Chelsea in January 1952. With a midweek afternoon kick-off, many of the children in front of the Spion Kop were given time off school especially for the occasion.

Harry Threadgold collects the ball under pressure from a Chelsea forward, watched by John Molyneux.

Threadgold comfortably retrieves the ball against Chelsea. In the background, many fans can be seen sitting on the wall in the corner at the Sealand Road end.

Morement, Threadgold and Lee defend another Chelsea attack. The Londoners eventually won the tie 3-2 after extra-time.

Rotherham-born Frank Brown points the way forward during pre-season training in 1952. There was a distinct Yorkshire feel to the squad in the early 1950s, with Pilkington, Dickens, Wright, Sutcliffe, Windle, Deakin and Morement all born in the white rose county.

Bill Deakin, George Pilkington, Geoff Coffin, Bill Jones and Billy Windle take a stroll down Sealand Road during pre-season training in 1952.

Inside left Bill Deakin gets in a cross during the first home game of the 1952/53 season, against York City. The game finished 1-1, with Chester's goal scored by Fred Richardson.

For the 1952/53 season, Chester switched from blue and white stripes to white shirts. This was the side that faced Tranmere Rovers in October. From left to right, back row: Ronnie Hughes, Ralph Morement, Dick Wright, Geoff Coffin, Ray Gill, Eric Lee. Front row: Bill Deakin, Don Travis, Fred Richardson, Norman Bullock, Billy Windle.

Louis Page meets the players for the first time after taking over from Frank Brown in 1953. From left to right, back row: Windle, Hughes, Thomas. Middle row: Lee, Travis, Coffin, Port. Front row: Gill, Rolfe, Fletcher, Whitlock, Sutcliffe, Wright.

A section of the crowd enjoying themselves at the Sealand Road end for the 1953 local derby against Wrexham.

Big Don Travis puts Wrexham goalkeeper Bob Connor under pressure in October 1953. Leading scorer Travis was on target in the 2-1 victory in front of 14,627 spectators.

Fred Sutcliffe prepares to challenge the Newport County goalkeeper in the Welsh Cup semi-final replay at Wrexham. Chester won the game 2-0, but were beaten by Flint Town United in the final. Although Chester reached the Welsh Cup final in three successive seasons in the mid-1950s, they were beaten on each occasion by non-League clubs – Rhyl, Flint and Barry.

CHESTER FOOTBALL CLUB, LIMITED

**Members of the Football Association, Ltd., The Football League Ltd., Div. III. (North),
Cheshire County Football Association, Cheshire County Football League and West Cheshire League**

President : T. SARL-WILLIAMS, Esq.

Chairman of Directors :-
S. ARGYLE, Esq.

Secretary :- W. P. Peters
Telephone - Ground 21048

Manager :- L. A. Page

Registered Office :-

" THE STADIUM,"

SEALAND ROAD,

CHESTER.

May 19th, 1955.

Dear Mr. Chairman,

At the end of March last, our position in the Northern League table was such that there appeared every prospect of our finishing the season reasonably clear of the last two positions. However, our hopes were sadly disillusioned when only 3 points were secured from the remaining 8 games, and whilst the re-election issue was a very keen fight involving 7 Clubs almost up to the final week of the season, it has resulted in our having to seek re-election.

This situation is most disappointing, particularly as the local interest in the Club is now comparable with that enjoyed when we were commanding a higher position in the league table, and not withstanding the unfortunate tendency for reduced support given to sporting activities our home game receipts are this season comparable with last. Furthermore as a result of the Directorate's recent convening of a Public Meeting, which was most enthusiastically received, a "100,000 Shillings Fund" was launched, the proceeds from which being essentially earmarked for retaining League Status football in the City, and this appeal is receiving a satisfactory response from the Public. A further development from this Meeting was the reconstituted Supporters' Association, whose membership is now 2408.

These acquisitions unfortunately came too late to assist the Club during the recent weeks; however the Board are confident that benefit will subsequently be derived therefrom thus enabling the management to develop the local playing talent which has been actively furthered during recent years and from which the senior team will benefit in the near future.

My Board view the necessity of seeking re-election with considerable concern, but, having submitted to you the considered prospects for the Club's future, we are sincerely hoping that you and your colleagues will be prepared to support our application for re-election, which is due for consideration at the meeting on June 4th next.

The sporting public of Chester with the Board are particularly anxious that League football status is retained in the City, and this is now only possible through the kindly and favourable considerations of yourselves and other Clubs of the 1st and 2nd Divisions, and we do earnestly seek your support, for which may we in anticipation of obtaining, convey our sincere thanks and gratitude.

Yours faithfully,

S. Argyle Chairman.

In 1955, Chester were forced to apply for re-election to the Football League for the second year in succession. Sam Argyle's letter to the other League chairmen did the trick and the club were comfortably re-elected.

Manager John Harris talks tactics to the players in summer 1957. The former Chelsea star was appointed player-manager in June 1956, but his astute management skills were quickly recognised and he moved on to Sheffield United in March 1958.

Billy Foulkes receives the Lancashire Cup from Jonathan Taylor of the Lancashire FA. Chester became the first club outside Lancashire to win the impressive trophy when they beat Burnley 1-0 in the 1958 final. Mickey Fields was the scorer of the goal.

Accrington Stanley goalkeeper Willie McInnes safely gathers a shot from Billy Foulkes as Norman Bullock rushes in. Chester's 5-1 victory, against the divisional runners-up, was the last game the club played in the Third Division (North).

Action from the 1958 Welsh Cup final, as the falling Barry Jepson beats Wrexham goalkeeper Billy Waters, only for his shot to go wide. The match finished 1-1, but Wrexham won the replay 2-1.

Four
Fourth Division Inertia
1958-1974

John Harris signs goalkeeper Ron Howells in September 1958, under the watchful eye of secretary Billy Peters. Howells, capped twice by Wales in 1954, joined the club from Worcester City, but continued to live and train in South Wales. He played 80 games for Chester, but was released in 1960 and joined Barry Town.

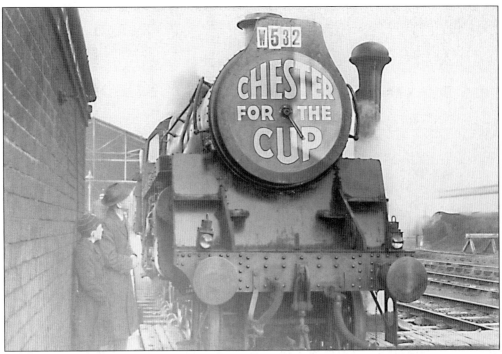

A special excursion train took Chester supporters to Mansfield for the FA Cup second round tie in December 1959. The train departed from Chester General station and the return fare was 11s.

Jimmy Anderson drops to the ground to avoid John Pimlott's shot, which flies into the net leaving Hartlepool goalkeeper Oakley stranded. This first home game of the 1960s finished 1-1, in front of 4,653 spectators.

Chester players line up before the Probables v. Possibles trial game in 1960, with the Probables playing in green shirts and the Possibles in blue and white stripes. From left to right, back row: Tony Wainwright, Frank Clempson, Jerry Ireland, Tommy Barrett, Johnny Anderson. Middle row: Eric Morris, Ray Griffiths, Billy Foulkes, Les Stopford, Colin Jones, Brian Biggins, Bill Brown, Walter Kelly, Jack Capper, John Watson, Ron Davies, George Spruce. Front row: Ray Gill, John Pimlott, Ronnie Hughes, Eric Raybould, Bobby Hunt, Jimmy Cooper, Alec Croft. Mystery surrounded the identity of the man in the number 3 shirt for the Possibles, who appeared as 'A.N. Other' in the programme. He was later revealed to be John Watson, an eighteen-year-old former Everton player, who was signed on the strength of his showing in the practice game. It proved to be a disastrous season for Chester and the club finished bottom of Fourth Division, a pattern that was repeated in the 1961/62 season. The early 1960s marked the end of an era as a number of players appeared in their final game for the club. Billy Foulkes played his last Chester game in April 1961, against Doncaster Rovers, after 296 appearances, while Chester's top two appearance record-holders, Ray Gill and Ronnie Hughes, both played their final game, against Carlisle United, in May 1962.

Chairman Sam Argyle symbolically lifts the first sod to make way for the erection of floodlights in July 1960. The cost of the floodlights was £16,000 – of which £10,000 was raised by the Chester FC Supporters Association. Watching closely, wearing the hat, is Supporters Association chairman Reg Moore.

Chester Football Club Limited,

THE STADIUM, SEALAND ROAD, CHESTER - Telephone : 2 1 0 4 8

Winners of The Football Association of Wales Challenge Cup 1908, 1933, 1947
The Lancashire Football Association Challenge Cup, 1957.   Cheshire Senior Cup 1895, 1897,
1904, 1908, 1909, 1931, 1932.   Cheshire County Bowl Competition 1933, 1935, 1937, 1940, 1944,
1945, 1946, 1954.   Cheshire County Football League 1921-22, 1925-26, 1926-27.

Members Football League Div., Cheshire County, West Cheshire and Chester & Dist. Leagues

President : **Y. Sari-Williams, Esq.**

Chairman : S. Argyle, Esq.   *Vice-Chairman :* R. W. Milton, Esq.
Directors : Messrs. J. H. Auckland, A. E. Cheshire, N. Clark,
W. A. Davies, A. C. Hall, G. S. Howarth, K. M. Jones, R. Rowlands,
F. H. Sullivan, C. Thompson.

Manager : **STANLEY C. PEARSON**   *Secretary :* **W. P. PETERS.**

FLOODLIGHT   FOOTBALL

Friday, April 14th, 1961

Kick-off 7-30 p.m.

THIRD LANARK

Frodsham Motors Limited

Agents :

Austin Cars and Commercials. Thorneycroft
Trucks. B.T.C Trailers.

Bridge Lane, Frodsham, Cheshire

Phone : Frodsham 3011/5.

Car Exchange (MOLD) Ltd.

KING STREET,
MOLD,
FLINTSHIRE.

Telephone No. 25344

W. E. ANFIELD

and Co., Ltd.

Wholesale and Retail Dealers in Oils, Paints,
Colours, Varnishes. Window Glass, Putty, etc.

Lower Bridge Street,
CHESTER

GIVE TO FIGHT

POLIO - NOW

National Fund for Poliomyelitis Research

Patron :
H.R.H. The Prince Phillip, Duke of Edinburgh, K.G, K.T.
Vincent House, Vincent Square, London, S.W.1

This Space has been generously donated by :-
Harry Williams & Co., Grosvenor Buildings,
12, Newgate Street, Chester.

WILLIAMS & MANSLEY

Printers and Stationers

Leadworks Lane (City Road Bridge),
Chester.   Phone 22141

CHESTER

★ CO-OPERATIVE ★

for all your

SPORTS EQUIPMENT

Make it a "WELL SAVED" Buy

with Dividend on all purchases

Official Programme 6d.

Chester Football Club Limited

At " The Stadium," Sealand Road, Chester.

Wed., Mar. 1st, 1961   **Kick-off 7-30 p.m.**

CONDITIONS OF SALE

This Ticket is issued subject to the rules
and regulations of the Football Association
and the Football League, and is allotted
on the distinct condition that no holder
thereof shall sell or transfer same for a
larger price than appears on the face
thereof. In the event of any breach of
this condition the Chester Football Club
Ltd., reserves the right to cancel this
ticket and to retain the money paid there-
for on allotment. Price of ticket will NOT
be returned in any circumstances if the
match has to be abandoned.

p.p. Chester F.C. Ltd.

Secretary

V.P. ENTRANCE E

Floodlight Football

Chester   v.
MANCHESTER
UNITED

Centre Stand 4/6

Nº B 005

This portion to be retained

Chester's floodlights were first used in the League Cup first round match against Leyton Orient in October 1960, with the 'official' switch-on taking place the following March for a prestigious friendly against Manchester United. Further flood-light friendlies took place against Scottish sides Third Lanark and Stirling Albion and German side Hamborn. Displayed here are a stand ticket for the Manchester United game and the cover of the official programme for the Third Lanark match.

Ron Davies challenges the Gillingham goalkeeper for the ball in the 1-1 draw between the sides in October 1961. Davies was one of the few successes of the season and, after scoring 44 goals in 94 games, was transferred to Luton Town for £12,200. He went on to have an illustrious career with Norwich City, Southampton, Portsmouth, Manchester United and Millwall, as well as playing for clubs in South Africa and America. A nimble player with good close control, he was mainly renowned for his tremendous heading ability, and his aerial prowess saw him win 29 international caps for Wales.

Former England internationals Raich Carter, the manager of Mansfield Town, and Chester's Stan Pearson met up to discuss old times before the League game between the sides in November 1961.

Chester players before the start of the 1963/64 season. From left to right, back row: McGill, Fitzgerald, Fleming, Read, Currie. Middle row: Randles (assistant secretary), Morris, Corbishley, Adams, Barton, Jones, Wheaton, Humes, Hauser (player-manager), Gardner (trainer). Front row: Peters (secretary), Bennion, Pritchard, Evans, Butler, McGowan, Starkey, Rowlands (chairman), Hall (director).

Alan Pritchard leaps to head Chester's first goal in the League Cup first round replay against Rochdale in September 1963. It proved to little avail, as Chester crashed to a 5-2 defeat.

Long-serving secretary Billy Peters retired in 1964 after thirty-three years with the club. Peters had initially been employed as a clerical assistant, by Charlie Hewitt, when Chester entered the Football League and had taken over as secretary on Alex Raisbeck's appointment in 1936.

Chester's all-conquering 'Famous Five' forward line scored 116 of Chester's 119 League goals in the 1964/65 season. Taking into consideration the FA Cup and League Cup, all five scored more than 20 goals. From left to right: Jimmy Humes (20 goals), Mike Metcalf (37 goals), Gary Talbot (35 goals), Hugh Ryden (20 goals), Elfed Morris (26 goals).

Gary Talbot watches the ball enter the net to put Chester into a 2-1 lead against Tranmere Rovers. The scorer, Mike Metcalf, is hidden by the Tranmere number 3, Eddie Robertson. Chester won the game 3-2.

In September 1964, supporters witnessed one of the most the most thrilling games seen at the stadium as Chester conquered Second Division Derby County 5-4 in the League Cup. Here, Mike Metcalf puts Chester on level terms at 2-2, after playing a delightful one-two with Gary Talbot.

With the score at 4-4, Man of the Match Metcalf saw his shot blocked by Derby 'keeper Reg Matthews ...

... but the ball broke loose to Gary Talbot, who chested it over the line as Metcalf checked for the offside flag.

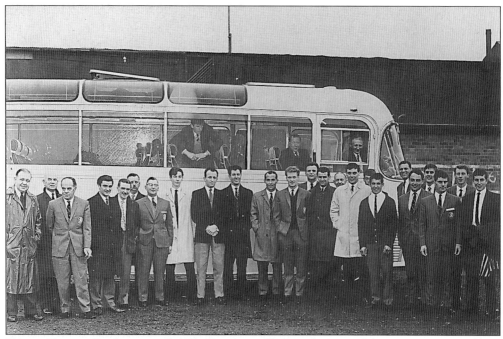

Trainer Tommy Gardner is in the driving seat as Chester players and directors prepare to leave for an away game from behind the old stand at Sealand Road.

Chairman Reg Rowlands struggles to give the players a free ride in the build-up to the FA Cup tie against Manchester United. Standing: Elfed Morris, Malcolm Starkey, Jimmy Humes, John Butler, Dennis Reeves, Dave Durie. Sitting: Mike Metcalf, Hugh Ryden. Rowlands, a fruit and vegetable merchant by occupation, was a popular and well-respected figure amongst the players.

Chester's FA Cup third round tie against Manchester United in January 1965 attracted plenty of media attention, and there were 45,660 spectators at Old Trafford to see if the minnows from the Fourth Division could cause an upset over the League Champions elect. Chester had reached the third round following victories over Crewe (5-0) and Barnsley (5-2). The Crewe game had included a hat-trick in under three minutes by Gary Talbot.

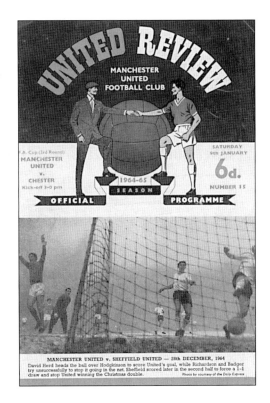

Chester got off to a flying start against Manchester United when Jimmy Humes (on the ground) sent a brilliant diving header past Dunne after only nine minutes. Chester retained the lead until early in the second half, when goals from Best and Kinsey gave the FA Cup favourites a narrow 2-1 victory.

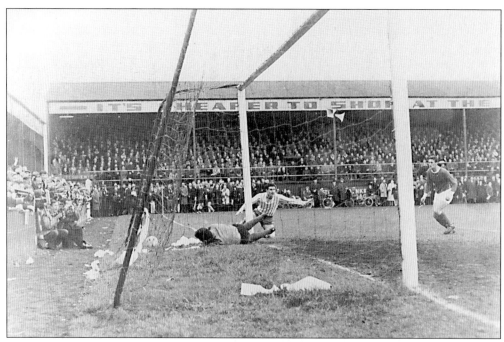

There were 14,782 spectators packed into the stadium to see Chester record one of their best results against local rivals Wrexham with a thrilling 6-1 victory in February 1965. Here, goalkeeper Fleet is beaten for the fifth time as winger Jimmy Humes completes his hat-trick.

The building of the Social Club was completed in three months at a cost of £14,000. It was initially run by the directors and the Supporters Association and was first used in June 1965.

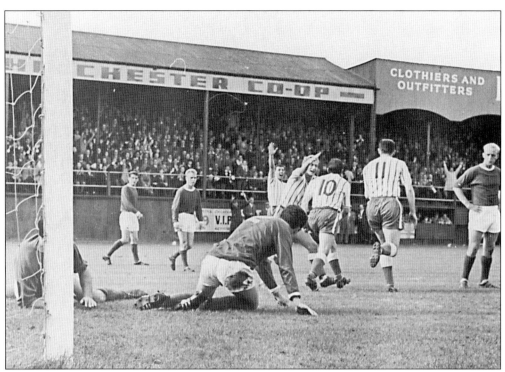

Hugh Ryden is first to congratulate Les Jones as he scores Chester's third goal in the 4-2 victory over Wrexham in September 1965.

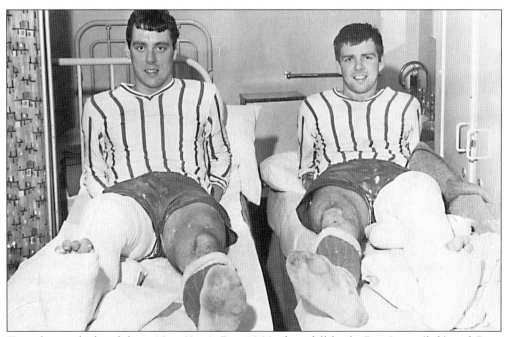

Tragedy struck the club on New Year's Day 1966 when full-backs Ray Jones (left) and Bryn Jones both broke their legs in a League fixture against Aldershot. On the same day, winger Garth Lee broke his leg playing for the reserves and one of the directors was killed in a car crash.

High jinx from the players in the swimming pool at the Norbreck Hydro Hotel in Blackpool before the FA Cup game against Newcastle in 1966.

The players and directors line up for the 1966/67 season. From left to right, back row: Pritchard (assistant trainer), H. Jones, Lea, Durie, Butler, Chadwick, L. Jones, Harley, Read, G. Bennett, Metcalf, Starkey, Harvey. Middle row: Chesworth (groundsman), Owen, Talbot, R. Jones, Holland, Humes, Berry, Reeves, Ryden, Sealey, Singleton, Morris, B. Jones, Burbridge, Gardner (trainer). Front row: Hauser (player-manager), Gandy (secretary), Horne, Auckland, Rowlands (chairman), Milton, Hall, Jones.

In 1967, Mike Metcalf and Mike Sutton embarked on a health food diet in an attempt to improve their fitness, much to the amusement of their colleagues.

Chairman Reg Rowlands and Peter Hauser greet Chester's new signing from Sheffield United, David Hancox, in summer 1967. Appearances were limited for the young Yorkshireman, who was competing for a forward place with Eddie Loyden, another new signing from Carlisle United. Peter Hauser remained as manager until February 1968 when he was sacked, leaving Chester lying in the Fourth Division re-election zone. The man chosen to replace him was Bradford Park Avenue assistant manager Ken Roberts.

Billy Dearden (left) and Gary Talbot are soaked by trainer Vince Pritchard after the last home game of the 1968/69 season, against Lincoln. The game proved to be Talbot's final match for the club after 83 goals in 154 League appearances. Dearden went on to join Sheffield United in 1970 for £11,000.

In 1969/70, Chester had their best FA Cup run since 1948 when they reached the fourth round. They were eventually beaten by Swindon Town after victories over Halifax Town, Doncaster Rovers and Second Division Bristol City. From left to right, back row: Ken Roberts (manager), Terry Bradbury, Graham Turner, Mike Sutton, Terry Carling, Nigel Edwards, Billy Dearden, Cliff Sear, Vince Pritchard (trainer). Front row: Derek Draper, Roy Cheetham, Keith Webber, Andy Provan, Graham Birks.

Manager Ken Roberts with Terry Bradbury, Albert Harley, Roy Chapman and Keith Webber in the summer of 1969. Roberts took over from Peter Hauser in March 1968. Ken Roberts is in the record books as the youngest player to feature in a Football League game. He was only 15 years and 158 days old when he played for Wrexham, against Bradford Park Avenue, in September 1951.

An uncomfortable pose for Roy Cheetham, Keith Webber and Alan Tarbuck. Nippy forward Tarbuck joined Chester from Crewe in 1969, and was transferred to Preston for £5,500 in October 1971 – an unpopular move with supporters.

An unusual team picture from the 1972/73 season. From left to right: John Taylor, Neil Griffiths, Ray Carter, Terry Owen, Geoff Davies, Graham Clapham, Nigel Edwards, Mick Hollis, John James, John Relish, Dave Pountney, Derek Draper, Dave Kennedy, Gordon Livsey, Paul Futcher, Graham Futcher, Bob Wallace, Ron Futcher.

Southampton defender John McGrath slides in to beat Derek Draper to the ball in the League Cup marathon of September 1972. Chester took their illustrious First Division opponents to three games before they were defeated 2-0 at neutral West Bromwich Albion. McGrath went on to become manager of Chester in January 1984.

Twins Ron (left) and Paul Futcher appeared together in a League fixture for the first time at Workington in October 1972 at the age of seventeen. A third Futcher, older brother Graham, also played for Chester in 1972, but never appeared in the same side as Paul or Ron.

In 1973, supporters were asked to choose a nickname for the club. Several fans thought 'The Seals' was an appropriate name for a side playing at Sealand Road. With a nickname chosen, the students of Chester College of Further Education Art School were asked to design a new club badge. The Seals badge was used in the programme and on the shirt until 1983, when the Chester City name was adopted and the Seals motif dropped.

Chester players prepare for the FA Cup third round tie against Aston Villa in January 1974 under the guidance of coach Brian Green. From left to right: Jimmy Redfern, Stuart Mason, Norman Whitehead, John James, Grenville Millington, Brian Green. The appointment of Green, in November 1973, marked a turning point in Chester's fortunes that ultimately led to promotion in 1975.

John James nods in the Chester equaliser in the Aston Villa cup tie. Chester were eventually beaten 3-1. James went on to finish leading scorer in 1973/74 with 23 league and cup goals.

Five
Goodbye Sealand Road
1974-1990

The Chester team that reached the semi-final of the League Cup and finally achieved promotion after fourty-four years in the Football League. From left to right, back row: Stuart Mason, Nigel Edwards, Trevor Storton, Grenville Millington, Reg Matthewson, John James, Tony Loska. Front row: Norman Whitehead, Ian Seddon, Derek Draper, Dave Lennard, Terry Owen.

It looks like a first strike of the season for Stuart Mason, but this goal against Swansea City, in November 1974, was in fact scored by the prostrate Derek Draper. The smiling John James also scored twice in a 3-0 victory.

CHESTER
FOOTBALL CLUB LTD.
1974-75

THE SEALS

CHESTER-FC

OFFICIAL PROGRAMME

Price

WEDNESDAY, NOVEMBER 13th, 1974
v
LEEDS Utd.
League Cup 4th Round
KICK-OFF 7-30 p.m.

10p

Chester were given little chance when they faced League Champions Leeds United at Sealand Road in the fourth round of the League Cup. The form book was turned on its head, however, as Chester swept three goals past a full-strength Leeds side. The Chester side that faced Leeds that night was Millington, Edwards, Loska, Storton, Matthewson, Mason, Whitehead, Seddon, Draper, James, Lennard.

John James puts Chester ahead in the League Cup tie against Leeds. His initial shot was blocked by 'keeper David Harvey, but James made no mistake when handed a second opportunity.

One of the key moments in the game was Grenville Millington's stunning first-half save from Terry Cooper, with the score at 1-0. After the interval, Trevor Storton and John James, from the penalty spot, extended Chester's lead.

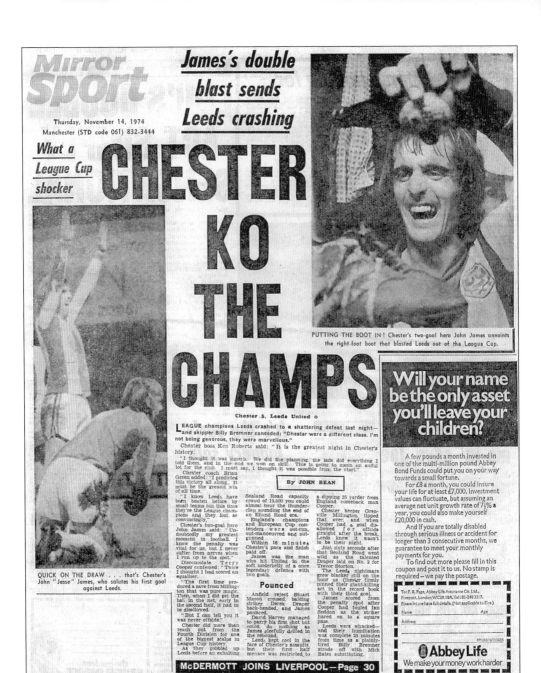

Mirror Sport

Thursday, November 14, 1974
Manchester (STD code 061) 832-3444

James's double blast sends Leeds crashing

What a League Cup shocker

CHESTER KO THE CHAMPS

PUTTING THE BOOT IN! Chester's two-goal hero John James anoints the right-foot boot that blasted Leeds out of the League Cup.

QUICK ON THE DRAW . . . that's Chester's John "Jesse" James, who salutes his first goal against Leeds.

Chester 3, Leeds United 0

LEAGUE champions Leeds crashed to a shattering defeat last night—and skipper Billy Bremner conceded: "Chester were a different class. I'm not being generous, they were marvellous."

Chester boss Ken Roberts said: "It is the greatest night in Chester's history.

"I thought it was superb. We did the planning, the lads did everything I told them, and in the end we won on skill. This is going to mean an awful lot for the club. I must say, I thought it was possible from the start."

Chester coach Brian Green added: "I predicted this victory all along. It must be the greatest win of all time.

"I know Leeds have been beaten before by small teams but this time they're the League champions and they lost so convincingly."

Chester's two-goal hero John James said: "Undoubtedly my greatest moment in football. I know the penalty was vital for us, but I never suffer from nerves when I run up to the spot."

Disconsolate Terry Cooper confessed: "Twice I thought I had scored an equaliser.

"The first time produced a save from Millington that was pure magic. Then, when I did get the ball in the net, early in the second half, it had to be disallowed.

"But I can tell you it was never offside."

Chester did more than reach out from the Fourth Division for one of the biggest scalps in League Cup history.

As they gobbled up Leeds before an exhalting

By JOHN BEAN

Sealand Road capacity crowd of 19,000 you could almost hear the thunderclap sounding the end of an Elland Road era.

England's champions and European Cup contenders were out-run, out-manoeuvred and out-gunned.

Within 16 minutes Chester's pace and finish paid off.

James was the man who hit United in the soft underbelly of a once legendary defence with two goals.

Pounced

Anfield reject Stuart Mason crossed, balding striker Derek Draper back-headed, and James pounced.

David Harvey managed to parry his first shot but could do nothing as James gleefully drilled in the rebound.

Leeds kept cool in the face of Chester's assaults but their first half menace was restricted to

a dipping 25 yarder from England comeback man Cooper.

Chester keeper Grenville Millington tipped that over, and when Cooper had a goal disallowed for offside straight after the break, Leeds knew it wasn't to be their night.

Just sixty seconds after Sealand Road went wild as the talented Draper laid on No. 2 for Trevor Storton.

The Leeds nightmare grew blacker still on the hour as Chester firmly pinned their giant-killing act in the record book with their third goal.

James scored from the penalty spot after Cooper had fouled Ian Seddon as the striker hared on to a square pass.

Leeds were whacked—and their humiliation was complete 20 minutes from time as a plainly-tired Billy Bremner strode off with Mick Bates substituting.

McDERMOTT JOINS LIVERPOOL—Page 30

Chester were given extensive national newspaper coverage following their dramatic 3-0 victory. This was the back page of the *Daily Mirror* the day after the game. It had been an incredible performance against a team brimming with internationals, who went on to reach the European Cup final later that season.

That man 'Jesse' James does it again. His 76th minute goal gave Chester a 1-0 victory in the League Cup fifth round replay against Newcastle United to put Chester into the semi-finals.

The linesman's flag is raised as Chester defend in force in the League Cup semi-final first leg against Aston Villa. Behind the main stand, the television cameras can be seen paying a rare visit to Sealand Road for recorded highlights on *Sportsnight*.

Terry Owen follows the ball into the net, as Gary Moore (on the ground) puts Chester on level terms for the second time.

Goalscorers Gary Moore and Terry Owen, together with Norman Whitehead, celebrate the 2-2 first leg draw with Villa. Chester were defeated 3-2 in the second leg at Villa Park, after a fighting performance which saw them pull back a two-goal deficit before succumbing to a goal ten minutes from time.

John James just fails to reach the ball before Exeter City goalkeeper Len Bond. Chester drew this game 1-1 in April 1975, their equaliser coming from Terry Owen late in the second half.

Stuart Mason squeezes a header past a Crewe defender to score one of the most crucial goals in the club's history. The solitary strike in the game at Gresty Road, the last game of the season, left Chester hoping that Lincoln would fail to pick up a point in their final match at Southport.

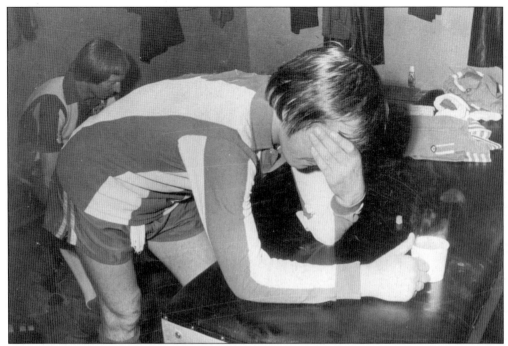

Tense moments for Tony Loska and Stuart Mason as they anxiously await the result of the Southport *v*. Lincoln City game. The players were in the Chester dressing room after playing in a charity game against the Cheshire Constabulary. Meanwhile, over at Haig Avenue, Southport won 3-2 to send Chester into the Third Division by .039 of a goal.

Chester players line up for the cameras before their first season in the Third Division. From left to right: Whitehead, Lennard, Edwards, Storton, Matthewson, Dunleavy, Seddon, Loska, Green (coach), Redfern, Mason, Owen, Daniels, Moore, James, Millington, Pugh, Draper. Barney Daniels, a £20,000 signing from Manchester City, had the honour of scoring the first goal in the Third Division.

Alan Oakes displays the Debenhams Cup after Chester's 4-3 aggregate victory over Port Vale in May 1977. The cup was contested between the two teams below the Second Division who had progressed the furthest in the FA Cup. Chester had reached the fifth round, where they had been unlucky to lose 1-0 to Wolves.

The Chester youth team in 1977/78 included a sixteen-year-old midfielder from Flint called Ian Rush. In April 1979, Rush made his full Chester debut, wearing the number 4 shirt, against Sheffield Wednesday. He went on to become one of the world's greatest strikers. The boys were in happy mood before their 9-1 defeat against Oldham Athletic in the Youth Cup third round. From left to right, back row: Dave Prestidge, Ian Rush, Kevin Higgins, Dave Jones, Dave Rowlands, Ian Edwards, Paul Needham, Stephen Ball. Front row: Gareth Eynon, Dave Gregory, Paul Lewis, Richie Gendall, Keith Massey.

Ian Mellor (right) puts Chester into a first-half lead against Swansea City in September 1978. Also in the picture are Ian Edwards (partially hidden) and Mark Nickeas. Edwards added a second, in the final minute, to give Chester a 2-0 victory.

Ian Edwards shields the ball from Norwich City's Martin Peters. Chester lost this League Cup third round game 2-0. In the previous round, the Seals had beaten First Division Coventry City 2-1. Three weeks after this game, Ian Edwards was awarded his second Welsh international cap when he played in the European Nations Cup tie against Malta at Wrexham. Wales won the game 7-0 and Edwards scored four of the goals, equalling the record for most goals in an international by a Wales player. Edwards went on to win a third Welsh cap, against West Germany, before moving to Wrexham in November 1979 for £125,000.

The future at Sealand Road . . .

With your help it's not a dream

In 1978, the club offered supporters the opportunity to buy a £200 repayable bond in order to help finance the building of a new stand. The accompanying brochure estimated the cost of the stand to be in excess of £250,000. In the event, the final cost proved to be double the initial estimate – creating a financial burden which ultimately led to the sale of the ground in 1990.

Chester players before the start of the 1979/80 season. From left to right, back row: Storton, Edwards, Rush, Zelem. Middle row: Howat, Jones, Burns, Matthews, Edwards, Cooke, Walker, Jeffries. Front row: Oakes, Sear, Henderson, Lloyd, Ruggiero, Raynor, Lewis, Gendall, Phillips, Sutcliffe. Confusingly, the squad included two players called Ian Edwards.

All heads are turned to watch Trevor Storton's spectacular shot enter the net in the 3-1 victory over Wimbledon in November 1979. The other Chester player in the picture is Ronnie Phillips.

Peter Sutcliffe hurdles a lunging tackle from Barnsley's Mick McCarthy, watched by Peter Henderson. Chester won this FA Cup second round tie 1-0, thanks to a last-minute penalty from Paul Raynor.

Ian Rush, Alan Oakes, Ronnie Phillips and Peter Henderson celebrate Rush's goal at Newcastle in Chester's 2-0 FA Cup third round victory. The youngster's tenth goal in twelve games brought him to the attention of a wider football audience and rumours circulated of a big money transfer to Liverpool or Manchester City. In the end it was Liverpool who signed him, in April 1980, for £300,000.

Brynley Jones heads Chester into a ninth-minute lead in the FA Cup fifth round match against Ipswich Town. The Suffolk side responded with goals from Burley and Wark just before half-time to go through 2-1. Chester's appearance in the last sixteen of the competition equalled their best-ever performance.

It's all smiles as Alan Oakes shows new signing Gary Simpson around the Stadium in the summer of 1981. Centre forward Simpson arrived in a £6,000 deal with Chesterfield and ended Chester's dismal 1981/82 relegation season as leading goalscorer with twelve.

A pre-season photograph from the 1981/82 relegation season: From left to right, back row: David Burns, Paul Raynor, Peter Zelem, Phil Harrington, John Cottam, Grenville Millington, Trevor Storton, Paul Needham, Steve Ludlam. Front row: Peter Sutcliffe, Trevor Phillips, Brynley Jones, Alan Oakes (player-manager), Gary Simpson, Ian Howat, Terry Cooke.

One of the most bizarre incidents to take place at Sealand Road occurred in a League Cup first round second leg match against Plymouth Argyle in September 1981. With the score at 2-2, Grenville Millington crashed into the goalpost making a save from Argyle's David Kemp. The post snapped at its base and, with no replacement available, the referee was forced to abandon the match. The photograph shows a dazed Millington walking along the goal line, while an amused Peter Sutcliffe watches Trevor Storton prop up the goalpost.

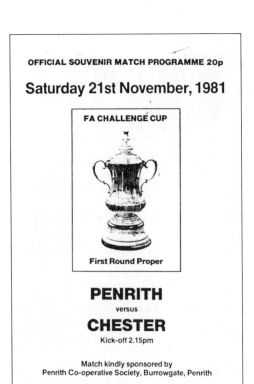

One of Chester's blackest days came in November 1981 when they were eliminated from the FA Cup by Penrith of the Northern League. The result had long-term repercussions as both chairman Reg Rowlands and manager Alan Oakes departed within a few months.

Penrith's Willie Armstrong challenges Grenville Millington for a cross. The ball ran free to Geoff Fell, who scored the only goal of the game.

Chairman Eric Barnes confirms Cliff Sear's appointment as manager, following the former youth-team coach's period in temporary control. Barnes himself had become chairman after purchasing a majority shareholding during the summer of 1982. Sear, a former Welsh international, had joined Chester from Manchester City in summer 1968 and served the club with distinction in a number of different roles. As youth team manager, he introduced many players into League football, including Ian Rush.

Although Chester finished ninety-second in the Football League in 1983/84, Andy Holden was rewarded with a Welsh international cap against Israel. The lion-hearted defender, who went on to play for Wigan and Oldham, would surely have added to this total had his career not been interrupted by a series of injuries.

Between the resignation of Cliff Sear in November 1982 and the arrival of Harry McNally in July 1985, Chester employed five different managers. John Sainty (top left), a former coach at Manchester City, served from November 1982 to November 1983. Long-serving defender Trevor Storton (top right) then took over as caretaker manager between November 1983 and the start of January 1984, while Cliff Sear briefly looked after the team before the appointment of former Port Vale manager John McGrath (bottom left) in January 1984. McGrath lasted less than twelve months and departed after a 5-1 defeat at Stockport County. He was replaced by midfielder Mick Speight (bottom right), who not only hauled Chester away from the re-election zone but also takes the credit for introducing Stuart Rimmer to the club.

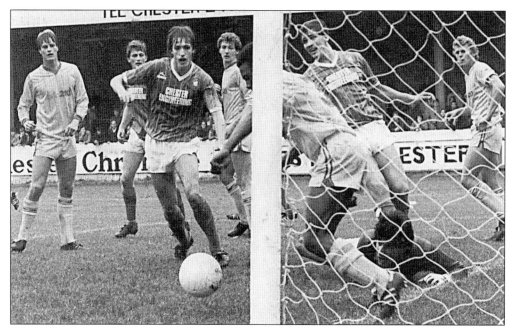

John Allen (partially hidden), Stuart Parker and Peter Zelem put pressure on the Reading defence in September 1983. Parker scored one of the goals in a 2-1 win – one of only seven victories in a campaign that saw Chester finish ninety-second in the Football League and gates sink below 1,000. The best results were once again achieved in the League Cup, where Chester pulled back a three-goal first round first leg deficit to beat Bolton Wanderers on penalties. In the next stage, Leeds United were beaten 1-0 at Elland Road before order was restored with the Yorkshire side's 4-1 victory at Sealand Road in the second leg.

It was John McGrath who signed nineteen-year-old Lee Dixon for Chester, on a free transfer from Burnley in 1983. McGrath predicted that Lee would win international honours. He was right. Lee moved on to Bury, Stoke City and Arsenal, and won 22 caps for England after playing 57 League games for Chester.

Chester's all-time leading goalscorer, Stuart Rimmer, joined the club from Everton in January 1985 and made an immediate impact with a hat-trick against Southend United. Within nine months the scouts were flocking to Sealand Road to watch a player who scored 32 goals in his first 42 games for the club. Sadly, Rimmer's season was cut short after he damaged his knee ligaments scoring against Orient in November. By 1987, he was back at his goalscoring best and, shortly after bagging a hat-trick against Gillingham, the popular striker moved to Watford for £210,000. 'Stuey' later played for Walsall and Barnsley before Harry McNally made him Chester's record signing at £94,000 prior to the second season in exile at Macclesfield. In 1992, he broke Gary Talbot's goalscoring record and only left Chester in 1998 after scoring 135 goals in 361 games. Fittingly, the master marksmen was on target in his final game for the club against Scarborough.

Peter Houghton (on the ground) and Andy Holden look to pick up the loose ball as Gary Bennett makes a desperate appeal for a goal in the 1-1 draw with Hartlepool United. It was Bennett's first home game after his arrival from Wigan, and he went on to make 254 appearances and score 63 goals in three separate spells for Chester.

John Kelly runs over to congratulate substitute Milton Graham on his goal against Tranmere Rovers in January 1986. Also in the picture is Gary Bennett. Talented midfielder Graham played 129 games for Chester before a £70,000 move to Peterborough United in summer 1989.

Ian Richardson sees his shot blocked by Rochdale 'keeper Dave Redfern in a 1-1 draw in February 1986. Richardson was signed from Watford for £15,000 as a replacement for the injured Stuart Rimmer.

GOING UP TO DIVISION III WITH CHESTER F.C. AND THE EVENING LEADER - APRIL 1986

Picture by MARK HIBBIN with the compliments of the Evening Leader,
Become a regular reader and get your copy delivered. Tel. Chester 48241

The *Chester Evening Leader* produced this card to celebrate promotion to the Third Division after a goal-less draw at Orient. The players celebrating are, from left to right, back row: Mickey Clarke (trainer), Steve Johnson, David Glenn, Bobby Coy, Ricky Greenhough, Martin Lane, John Butcher, Peter Houghton. Front row: Milton Graham, John Kelly, Earl Barrett, Ian Richardson, Gary Bennett.

Captain Andy Holden scores the club's first goal in the Third Division for four years with a penalty in the 2-2 draw with Carlisle United. Both teams finished with ten men as Graham Abel was sent off for Chester.

Stuart Rimmer slides the ball home for Chester's only goal in a 2-1 home defeat by Middlesbrough in May 1987. The Boro defender on the right is Gary Pallister.

Graham Barrow and Bolton defender Mark Came (to the right of Barrow) watch David Felgate punch the ball clear in the mud and snow at Sealand Road. When Barrow became manager, in 1992, Came became one of his first signings, while Felgate joined Chester in October 1993. The game itself, perhaps unsurprisingly given the conditions, finished goal-less.

Chester finished the 1988/89 season in eighth position, their highest placing since 1977/78. From left to right, back row: Stuart Walker (physiotherapist), Graham Abel, Barry Butler, Ian Benjamin, Chris Lightfoot, Billy Stewart, Steve Johnson, Joe Hinnigan, Gary Bennett, Colin Woodthorpe. Front row: Carl Dale, David Glenn, Graham Barrow, Harry McNally (manager), Milton Graham, Joe Jakub, Sean Lundon.

Carl Dale is stretchered off the field during the home game against Fulham in September 1989. It was a change of fortune for Dale, who had scored a hat-trick against the same club the previous season in a resounding 7-0 victory. Dale was leading scorer in each of his three seasons at Chester, before an £82,000 transfer to Cardiff City in August 1991.

Full-back Colin Woodthorpe tries to intercept a cross from Tranmere's Johnny Morrissey in a Leyland DAF quarter-final match at Prenton Park. Woodthorpe was transferred to Norwich City for £225,000 at the end of the 1989/90 season after 155 League games for Chester.

In November 1989, Chester fans were left reeling as it was revealed that the Sealand Road ground had been sold with vacant possession. Ironically, the announcement was made on the verge of Chester's FA Cup tie at Macclesfield, their home for the next two seasons.

Ray Croft, standing in the centre of the picture, took over as chairman in March 1990 after the majority shareholding passed to property developers Morrisons. Croft's first task was to find a home for the 1990/91 season. On the left of the picture is secretary Albert Eckersley.

Graham Abel heads home Brian Croft's corner to score the final goal at Sealand Road. The 2-0 victory, against Rotherham United, also secured Chester's place in the Third Division.

The sign says 'EXIT' and the clock shows 4.45 p.m. as Chester players Graham Barrow, Carl Dale, Robbie Painter, David Hamilton, Chris Lightfoot and Graham Abel leave the Sealand Road pitch for the last time.

An emotional end to eighty-four years at Sealand Road as the supporters give a standing ovation to the players after the Rotherham game. The graffiti on the main stand leaves no doubt who Chester fans blamed for the sale of ground. In April 1990, they still had no idea where they would be watching home games the following season.

Chester players take the applause of the fans after the Rotherham game. From left to right: David Pugh, Brian Croft, Harry McNally (manager), Robbie Painter, Carl Dale, Billy Stewart, Martin Lane, Alan Reeves, Barry Butler, Chris Lightfoot, Graham Abel, David Hamilton, Colin Woodthorpe and Gary Bennett.

Six
Out of the League
1990-2001

Following the sale of Sealand Road in 1990, Chester played their home games at the Moss Rose in Macclesfield. Subsidised transport was laid on by the club for the eighty-mile round trip.

Carl Dale shoots for goal against Arsenal's David Seaman in the Rumbelows Cup second round first leg game at Moss Rose in September 1990. Arsenal won the game 1-0 in front of 4,135 spectators.

Chester players leave the field at Highbury following a 5-0 defeat in the second leg. From left to right: Neil Morton, Carl Dale, Chris Lightfoot, Brian Croft, Neil Ellis, Barry Butler, Roger Preece, Alan Reeves and Martin Lane.

An unusual view of Barry Butler, in goal at Bradford City, in October 1990. Butler had taken over from Billy Stewart, who had been sent off after only sixteen minutes. Also in the picture are Martin Lane and Graham Abel. Between them, the three players made more than 800 appearances for the club.

The legendary Harry McNally in reflective mood after seeing Billy Stewart and David Pugh sent off in a goal-less first half at Bradford City. Chester lost this controversial game 2-1.

Graham Abel blasts home a penalty at the Star Lane end in an FA Cup tie against Leek Town in December 1990. Chester won this second round replay 4-0. It was a short trip for the non-League side, who only had to travel twelve miles down the A523 for the game. This helped swell the attendance to 2,420 – a good crowd for a midweek game at Moss Rose.

Number 10 Gary Bennett scores the equaliser at Maine Road in the Rumbelows Cup against Manchester City. Chester eventually lost this second round first leg tie 3-1. The second leg was played at Edgeley Park, Stockport because of safety concerns over Moss Rose, and the Manchester side completed a 6-1 aggregate victory.

Billy Stewart is chaired off the field after the final game at Moss Rose, against Leyton Orient, in May 1992. The 1-0 victory also ensured Chester's survival in Division Two.

Chester's revival in the second half of the 1991/92 season coincided with the news that work had finally begun on constructing the Deva Stadium. The 6,000 capacity ground was built in thirty weeks and opened against Stockport County on 25 August 1992.

Barry Butler, Stuart Rimmer and Graham Barrow celebrate Eddie Bishop's goal in a 3-1 defeat by Leyton Orient in January 1993. There was little to cheer in City's first season at the Deva Stadium and the club were relegated after losing 33 of their 46 games. It proved a difficult start in management for Graham Barrow, who had taken over from his mentor, Harry McNally, in October 1992.

Graham Barrow did a tremendous job in building a squad that bounced straight back to Division Two as runners-up to Shrewsbury Town in 1993/94. From left to right, back row: Berry, Greenall, Pugh, Stewart, Leonard, Moss, Whelan. Middle row: Allen (secretary), Donnelly, Thompson, Bishop, Wheeler, Jenkins, Rimmer, Limbert, Hinnigan (physiotherapist). Front row: Jakub, Lightfoot, Crofts (chairman), Barrow (player-manager), Came, Preece.

Dave Thompson shoots for goal in the League game against Mansfield Town in February 1994. Thompson's exciting wing play was a key feature of the 1993/94 promotion team.

Graham Lancashire celebrates his 88th-minute winner against Preston North End in one of the most dramatic games seen at the Deva Stadium. The loan signing from Burnley was on target twice as Chester recovered a 2-1 deficit to win 3-2 and virtually secure promotion. The official attendance of 5,638 was a record League attendance for the Deva Stadium.

Happy times as Graham Barrow celebrates promotion in May 1994, flanked by centre-backs Colin Greenall and Mark Came. Within three months, Barrow had left the club after the board had refused to give him enough backing to build for the future.

Another new era dawned following the departure of Graham Barrow in summer 1994. Mike Pejic was appointed manager, with Kevin Ratcliffe as his assistant. By January 1995, Chester were bottom of Division Two, having only won three games, and Pejic was dismissed following a 4-0 home defeat by York City. The appointment of Derek Mann as manager, followed by Ratcliffe, failed to turn round the club's fortunes and the club were relegated with five games of the season remaining. The final total of six victories was the lowest since joining the League.

Drama at the Racecourse Ground as Eddie Bishop becomes the second Chester player to be dismissed in the first 45 minutes in the 2-2 draw with Wrexham in February 1995.

Gary Shelton, Don Page and Jason Burnham take the applause of the Chester fans after Andy Milner's late goal had given nine-man Chester an unlikely point at Wrexham.

Cyrille Regis' classic header, from a Neil Fisher free-kick, puts Chester into the lead against Hereford United in September 1995. Regis inspired some excellent team performances at the start of the 1995/96 season, even though his injury problems meant he rarely completed a full 90 minutes.

Two footballing legends, Peter Jackson and Cyrille Regis, both celebrated their 600th Football League appearances in the 1995/96 season.

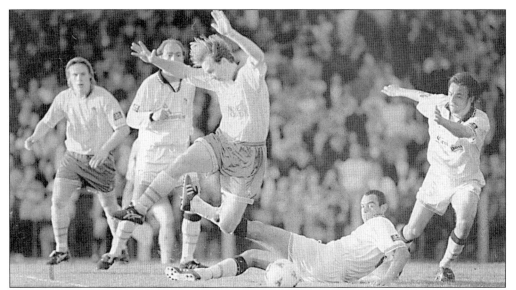

Chris Priest crashes to the ground under a tackle from Swansea City's Joao Moreira in the second leg of the play-off match at the Vetch Field. Chester had reached the 1997 play-offs after finishing sixth in Division Three. Following a goal-less draw at the Deva Stadium, Chester had travelled to South Wales as the underdogs, and Priest's first-half dismissal left the Blues with an uphill struggle. In the end, Swansea were comfortable 3-0 victors.

In October 1998, Chester went into administration after owner Mark Guterman failed in his attempts to sell the club. The Chester City Independent Supporters Association were at the forefront of efforts to rescue the club, not only raising thousands of pounds but also increasing public awareness of Chester's plight. In January 1999, Chester's match against Brighton was televised live on Sky and the ISA arranged the third 'Fans United' day, at which football fans from all over the country were invited to attend. Blackpool and Lincoln City fans were among those present.

Supporters gather on the pitch after the final game of the 1998/99 season against Rotherham United. With the club still in administration, there was a widespread belief that the game was the last in the club's history. During the summer, however, American Terry Smith stepped in to buy the club and promised a bright future.

Chester players line up for the final season in the Football League in 1999/2000. From left to right, back row: Lancaster, A. Shelton, Wright, Conkie, Cutler, Brown, Ajet, Beckett, Blackburn. Middle row: Hinnigan (physiotherapist), Doughty, Kilgannon, Woods, Cooper (coach), Berry, Rendall, Moss, Cross, G. Shelton (coach). Front row: Carson, Jones, Fogg (coach), Richardson, Smith (manager), Fisher, Davidson. Terry Smith had taken over as manager following Kevin Ratcliffe's departure after only three games, despite having had no experience of either managing or playing football at any reasonable level. With a background in American football, Smith argued that coaching was much the same in any sport. One of his first actions was to appoint a captain of defence, midfield and attack.

124

It's all going horribly wrong. Physio Joe Hinnigan sums up the feelings of all the supporters as Chester crash to a 7-1 home defeat against Brighton on 26 February. The result was Chester's worst home defeat in the Football League.

The moment when survival became a possibility. Ian Atkins celebrates a 2-1 victory at Leyton Orient on 15 April. Carl Heggs and Neil Fisher were the goalscorers in front of the most vociferous away support for many seasons. By the middle of April, the 'Great Escape' had gathered momentum as Chester lost only two of the next ten games following the Brighton debacle. Atkins had taken over as manager from Terry Smith at the start of January, when the team had looked dead and buried following heavy defeats against relegation rivals Leyton Orient and Carlisle United.

Luke Beckett feels the frustration as another chance goes begging in the final game of the season against Peterborough United. Chester had only required one point from the last two games to survive in the League. Unfortunately, a 1-0 defeat at Cheltenham had left them still seeking that elusive point when Peterborough visited the Deva Stadium on 6 May.

The goal that ended sixty-nine years of Football League membership. Wayne Brown can only look on in anguish as Peterborough fans celebrate Richie Hanlon's goal in the 64th minute. The 1-0 defeat – coupled with victory for Shrewsbury at Exeter and a narrow loss for Carlisle at Brighton – consigned Chester to non-League football by a margin of two goals. The 'Great Escape' had failed at the final hurdle.

Total despair for the supporters as the reality of relegation begins to sink in.

Stuart Hicks and a distraught young fan try to come to terms with Chester's relegation. Few players have made such a big impression in such a short period of time as Hicks, who only made thirteen appearances in a Chester shirt after joining the club from Leyton Orient. Hicks seemed to symbolise the fighting spirit engendered in both the fans and the players for the final few games of the season and the likeable centre half became a huge hero with the supporters. In the end it was to no avail, but most people felt that the damage had been done before Ian Atkins had taken control, when Terry Smith had taken his disastrous decision to manage the team.

An unused ticket for the final Football League game, against Peterborough United.

Angus Eve became Chester's most capped international player in 2000, despite only ever appearing in 14 League games for the club. The Trinidad & Tobago international played 35 games for his country while registered as a Chester player. He joined City in December 1999 but was frequently unavailable for club duties because of international commitments. After making 11 appearances for his country in 1999/2000, he was loaned back to his former club in Trinidad, Joe Public, following relegation and won a further 24 caps in the 2000/2001 season. His contract with Chester ended in summer 2001.

Chester players celebrate the club's first cup win in twenty-four years after victory in the Nationwide Variety Club Trophy final at Kingstonian in May 2001. Chester won the final 4-2 on penalties after 120 minutes of goal-less football.